UNEXPECTED SUBJECTS

Hau Books are published by the
Society for Ethnographic Theory (SET)

www.haubooks.org

Essays in Ethnographic Theory

The ethnographic essay provides a creative form for new work in anthropology. Longer than a journal article, shorter than a conventional monograph, ethnographic essays are experiments in anthropological thought, probing particular cases, topics, or arguments, to propose in-depth but concentrated analyses with unusual insight. In the past these were often published by research institutes or academic departments, but in recent years the style has enjoyed less space than it deserves. Hau Books is pleased to offer room for renewing the essay as an anthropological genre. Our Essays in Ethnographic Theory are published as short books, in print, ebook, and open-access PDF editions.

UNEXPECTED SUBJECTS

Intimate Partner Violence, Testimony, and the Law

Alessandra Gribaldo

HAU Books
Chicago

Cover image: Chiara Fumai, "God Save It", collage and embroidery on Konstantin Raudive's 'Breakthrough', 31 x 21 cm, 2014 (detail). Courtesy of The Church of Chiara Fumai.

Cover design: Daniele Meucci and Ania Zayco
Layout design: Deepak Sharma, Prepress Plus
Typesetting: Prepress Plus (www.prepressplus.in)

ISBN: 978-1-912808-30-4 [paperback]
ISBN: 978-1-912808-73-1 [ebook]
ISBN: 978-1-912808-34-2 [PDF]
LCCN: 2020950104

Hau Books
Chicago Distribution Center
11030 S. Langley
Chicago, Il 60628
www.haubooks.org

Hau Books is printed, marketed, and distributed by The University of Chicago Press.
www.press.uchicago.edu

Printed in the United States of America on acid-free paper.

Contents

Acknowledgments ix

Introduction 1
Methods and Caveats 5
Overview 9

Chapter 1. (Un)familiar Violence 13
Violence Degree Zero 13
Mistreated Subjects and Intractable Violence 23

Chapter 2. Wavering Intentions 35
Recognize and Speak the Violence! 35
Maltrattamenti in Famiglia and the Abused Subject 47
The Experience of Intimate Partner Violence: A Crime with a Story 54

Chapter 3. Confessing Victimhood 67
Evidence and Testimonial Proof 67
The Burden of Evidence: Experience 73
When Evidence Lies in the Victim Subject 82

Chapter 4. The Gender of True-Lying 93

The Burden of Persuasion: Intention and Biased Evidence 93

Agency vs Credibility 100

Oblique Narratives: The Imperfect Victim 109

Conclusions 125

References 133

Acknowledgments

This work would never have seen the light of day without the support of the Independent Social Research Foundation (ISRF), which granted me an Independent Scholar Fellowship between 2016 and 2017. In particular, I wish to thank Louise Braddock and Charles Stewart.

A special thank you is due to Giuditta Creazzo, to the *Casa delle donne* in Bologna, and to the professionals and lawyers who work there. This contribution does not address their daily work, or the feminist intelligence of their practices. Some of them might not agree with what I write, and others will find it incredibly trivial or banally illegible. I tried to report something that they already know very well; therefore, I started from their comments on their own work, and their capacity to use and dismantle the professional language of victimhood.

Prior versions of some of the material in this book appeared in *American Ethnologist* (2014), *Anuac: Journal of the Italian Society of Cultural Anthropology* (2019), and *PoLAR: Political and Legal Anthropology Review* (2019).

I thank the three anonymous reviewers for their constructive insights, and Hylton White, from Hau Books, for his kindness and accurate work. Thanks to Ilaria Vanni and Giovanna Zapperi for their invaluable comments on a first version of the manuscript; Simonetta Gribaldo, without whose constant support and advice I would neither have started nor finished writing this book; Lino, for always being there; and Agata, who agreeably and regularly interrupted my work.

And finally, I wish to thank the women I met during my research—those who were willing to talk and those who "would prefer not to."

Introduction

But after all, isn't truth-telling also embedded in the dense and complex tissue of ritual? It too has been accompanied by numerous beliefs, and accorded strange powers. So perhaps there is an entire ethnology of truth-telling to be pursued.
Michel Foucault, 2014

Intimate partner violence, in its disturbing recurrence, is an often undertheorized issue. To take it into account through an anthropological approach allows us to place it within a broader debate on gendered subjectivity, power, and agency. It also means addressing the peculiar relations among the social acknowledgment of the phenomenon, the act of denouncing violence, and the subjective experience of the violent acts perpetrated by the intimate partner. Diverse feminist traditions share the aim of creating possibilities for talking about and denouncing violence. Re-entering language is one of the main strategies used to help victims of intimate partner violence and to facilitate their recovery. The political act of breaking the silence interpellates women to talk, to take a position, to express themselves and, by doing so, to name violence. This discourse of the therapeutic power of narrating, which can also be found in anthropological works on violence (Jean-Klein and Riles 2005: 178-179), is what primarily identifies women as subjects who must speak out and tell their story.

The feminist practice of dialogue involving peers and advocates is a powerful tool in linking the personal to the political, by invoking a shared public space in which to recognize individual violence within a social horizon of meaning. This spreading of personal narratives of violence into the public context entails that institutions recognize domestic violence as a social issue. The process of identifying intimate partner violence raises the question of whether a victim is able to express the act itself in her own voice, and of how intelligible and persuasive her voice is in the institutional context. How can violence in intimate relationships be made present to institutions? How is the abused subject constituted in front of them? What requirements relate to her ability to identify and denounce the violent act?

Speaking in legal terms has a decisive, effective, and symbolic value in the definition of victimhood. Moving into an institutional dimension is perceived as a milestone that acknowledges that violence has been perpetrated, that the testimony of this violence is truthful, and that women are political subjects. The pressure on the victim of domestic violence to speak about the factual events, about herself and her relationship with the perpetrator, and to denounce him before the law, has vast implications. Literature on gendered violence and the law has shown how the victim's experience of violence is exacerbated by the systemic violence of the socio-legal order. A trial proceeds according to its own internal logic, from the opening statement to the judge's ruling, obscuring the particularities of crime in intimate contexts and rejecting the ambiguity produced at the intersection of intimacy and violence, as well as the material implications of power imbalances (Boiano 2015).

These dynamics are evident in the court's demands for truthfulness in the testimony of women who have experienced violence. In a context where documentary evidence is often not available, women's testimonies play an essential role. In the absence of documentation from emergency room visits or statements from witnesses, evidence is in fact often based exclusively on the testimony of the victim. This is the main means of establishing proof, so much so that it may represent the only element upon which a judgment is based, provided the testimony has achieved a suitable degree of validity. To narrate one's own experience in recognizable terms within the public space is neither easy nor something that can be taken for granted. Declaring an experience of violence means claiming rights and invoking change through reference to one's personal history. Testifying to domestic violence entails the risk of being marginalized, judged excessive, seen as playing victim, and thought of as manipulative: women do not speak, speak too little or too much, their testimonies are paradoxical in their very constitution, characterized by an inadequate and contradictory structure. In recent years, violence against women has received growing attention in Italy. Gender violence has increasingly become a political issue, as shown by successes among the youngest generations of the feminist grassroots movement *Non Una Di Meno* (Not One Less). The need to speak out against violence, and to speak with respect for women's will, are widely discussed in the movement and in feminist debate. The idea of 'femicide' has gained momentum with reports in different media on instances of gendered violence that resulted in women being injured or killed. At the same time, the over-exposure of femicide matches with an invisibility of domestic violence.

This short book extends ideas I have developed in recent articles (Gribaldo 2014, 2019a, 2019b). Using Italy as an illustrative case, I theorize the problematic encounter among the necessity to speak, the entanglement of violence and intimacy, the subjectivity implied, and the way the law takes on domestic violence. I show how diverse ways of articulating experience are required in different professional fields such as social services, law enforcement, and the justice system. These ways include speaking the facts, giving the reasons, telling the truth, talking about one's self, taking a clear stance, claiming one's rights, and pressing charges. This collection of different modalities of bearing witness is what I call *speaking violence*, so as to capture both the topic of what is spoken and the performative violence of the request for a narration in an institutional context. When a woman presses charges and then drops them, not wishing to incriminate her violent husband, what does she want? What is the nature of this silent, ambivalent, and contradictory subject? What duplicity is 'concealed' behind the actions of a woman who seeks to claim compensatory damages from her ex-partner/husband, or to gain sole custody of their children? How can we view a subject who presses charges and then proves incapable of expressing the accusation, other than as 'suspect' or at least pathologically 'lacking'? More generally, I wish to analyze the space for speaking, testimony, and ultimately the victim's subjectivity. Is there a real opportunity to tell the truth about gender violence, to speak about one's own experience in front of institutions? Beyond the acknowledged hardship that women who press charges are confronted with, is there an inner difficulty that lies in the status of testimonial proof when gender, intimacy, and violence are at stake? In what ways does the juridical truth regime imply specific modalities for linking manifestations of truth and the speaking subject? In what ways is the obligation to tell the truth connected to the obligation to investigate the self as an object of knowledge? Finally, what role does gender play in these practices?

I contend that a two-fold strategy is needed to address these questions. First, rather than asking what abused women want from the law, it may be more productive to understand what the law wants from women. Second, it would be more constructive to consider the relationship between professionals and victims of violence as an encounter between two *hesitations*. Even if it is sufficiently clear what women are asking for in their daily life—that is, a life without violence—their relationship with the law in addressing institutions, and the response by the justice system, emerge as exceptionally opaque. This opacity comes from the problematic relationship between the demonstration of violence, intimacy, and gender. The tension between institutional devices and agency becomes particularly significant in the case of victims of domestic violence, thus allowing us to delve into the process of "seeing broad principles in parochial facts" (Geertz 1983: 167). If women hesitate before the law, the justice system, for its part, shows as many reluctances and failures, as much embarrassment and difficulty, in making domestic violence an appropriate object of judgement. An ethnography of the construction of witness testimony is central to my analysis. This focuses on the modalities of interpellation and the procedures of legitimation required of a *teste,* a witness, who is also a victim. The uncertain status of witnessing raises diverse doubts and questions for anthropological thought. An ethnographic analysis of the dynamics that produce the subjectivity of the victim in the institutional context sheds light not only on the ways in which the Italian legal system essentially (re)produces the conditions of violence against women (the secondary victimization), but also on the conundrums that make women unexpected subjects for the law. The meanings of responsibility, autonomy, and agency can be deployed by considering forms of social life and personhood that do not fit categories of power, cause, and effect in the way the law expects. My wish is to connect feminist issues, especially the long-debated disavowal of women's words, with questions that anthropology is good at answering—and possibly to pose new ones.

Methods and Caveats

My ethnography in Italy was carried out as part of a wider action-research project financed by the European Union (through the *Istituto di Ricerca Cattaneo* in Bologna) and entitled *Why Doesn't She Press Charges? Understanding and*

Improving Women's Safety and Right to Justice. This project was led by criminologist Giuditta Creazzo and was designed to analyze the relationship between women who have suffered domestic violence and the judicial system in Italy, the United Kingdom, Spain, and Romania (Creazzo 2013). Interviews were thus carried out in each national context with both women victims of violence accessed through shelters and with different categories of professionals working within the health, legal, and social management of domestic violence. Observations were also made in court in order to report dynamics during trials. My research in the city of Bologna was carried out in collaboration with the *Casa delle donne per non subire violenza*, a women's anti-violence shelter. I conducted observations of twenty-five public hearings on familial abuse in criminal court in Bologna, and twenty interviews with women at the city's women's shelter, between June 2010 and December 2011. To observe a specific hearing, scheduled for a given day, meant spending quite some time in court because of delays and postponements. Hanging around, chatting with witnesses, and listening to hearings on diverse crimes, all gave me a chance to better understand the peculiarities of domestic violence trials. All the in-depth interviews, from one and a half to three hours long, focused primarily on the legal aspects of cases. However, the interviews also left space for narratives about relationships with partners, the paradox of a system at the same time meddling and ineffectual, and the context of common judgment on the victim. The voices of abused women that I collected through my interviews are of people who were presented to me as 'having undertaken a path' and therefore as being willing to talk of their experience with a researcher. In addition, together with Giuditta Creazzo, twenty-one interviews were conducted in the Bologna district with professionals involved in the management of domestic violence cases: nine magistrates (public prosecutors and judges), a lawyer, the director of a local emergency room, six professionals working at the city's anti-violence center and social services, and four police officers. The focus of these interviews was on the relevant and recurring issues in legal assistance and safety during the management of domestic violence cases, and on the dynamics of legal proceedings and trials. Interviews and observations in court were carried out over the same period, an overlapping which highlighted the contrast between the professionals' narratives and what happened in the court, as well as between the women's statements inside and outside of court.

The interviews with social workers and the police produced contradictory images of battered women: they are ambivalent victims, they don't know what they want, they are evasive, they are intimidated, they are strategic. Those with legal professionals highlighted the lack of evidence, the centrality of statements, and the need to be persuaded. The ethnographic work captured the ambiguous clues within legal rationales regarding the statement on the violence suffered and the consequent judgment on the accused: the silences of the women in court and within institutions, the perplexed glances between the judge and the public prosecutor when faced with these silences, the embarrassed smiles of the judges, the sighs of the social assistants. In the end, the overall question asked by the action research—why does she not press charges?—may even sound rhetorical. The percentage of women who do not press charges is so large that it would definitely be more effective to ask instead the opposite: why *does* she press charges for partner violence? Not only is it often an unpunished crime, but it is also a crime that is rarely charged. More often than not, when charges are made, the cases are not attributable to the definition of the crime of familial abuse. The contrast between the growing attention of the media and institutions and the very few court cases for domestic abuse is striking. I identified a space in which different registers and perspectives, different readings and expectations about gender and the victim, intersect—creating, as my research proceeded, more questions than answers. I continued to frequent the *Casa delle donne* in the years following the research, through various collaborations, allowing more or less informal exchanges and conversations on the questions raised.

My reflections arise from the impossibility of finding a single lens for reading the phenomenon, combined with the desire to maintain a feminist vision and at the same time an anthropological sensibility, in order to take note of the silences beyond the words spoken by women victims of violence, as well as of the hesitations that they face from institutions. This book does not aim at treating the relation between law and the crime of domestic violence in Italy, nor to problematize the theme of domestic violence in anthropology. It is rather an ethnographic interweaving of the threads of intimate violence, gender, voices, and the law. The notions of intimacy, consent, experience, awareness, evidence, and testimony are the most productive in tackling a number of issues that arise when dealing with this kind of violence in institutional settings.

I have not approached juridical dynamics by setting them within the specific Italian context, nor through an introduction to domestic violence within and outside the court, nor by following the proceedings. In this text there is not much reference to context; the biographical, individual trajectories that make the response to violence and to justice specific for each woman are not reported or singled out. This is due to various reasons. First, I have tried to respect the anonymity of the women who agreed to speak, and of those who found themselves giving testimony in court. Second, my work could not address the imponderable diversity of women victims. Why one woman decided to press charges and invited me to go with her to a TV program to speak out, whereas another told me her story in a whisper, wondering what might ever lead a woman to press charges, was not straightforwardly correlated to class, origin, condition, level of violence, or family history. Rendering the meaning and consequentiality of these stances exceeded my capacity for analysis and was not the aim of my project, which was limited to exploring some recurring issues emerging from my own ethnographic observations. A third and more methodological issue lies in my interest in giving a picture of what is said and what is judged through the social life of words within the institutional space, engaging ethnographically with accounts of domestic violence as crudely as they emerge in the space of Italian courts. I was interested in rendering the play among different institutional rationales, and the (always partial) erasure of any possible reference to relations of power when judgement was at stake. Keeping ethnography *suspended* seemed to me the best way to allow for the emergence of certain logics of telling, of possibilities for speaking and for judging, that address specific theoretical issues and allow for the meaning and representation of violence to become a space for reflection.

Rather than an anthropology *of* something, this essay is an anthropological reflection that stands between something and something else: an ethnography of institutional devices that focuses on the encounter between women's words and what the law requests in the context of intimate partner violence, the eliciting of intelligible subjectivities and practices of resistance and, concurrently, a reflection on evidence, persuasion, and testimony. If a property of evidence—in law as in anthropology—is that it be free of human intention, then a reflection on intention, persuasion and expectation, through unexpected voices and silences, may contribute to a new sense of "getting it right" (Hastrup 2004) in legal and anthropological knowledge.

Overview

In what follows, Chapter One is a conceptual exploration of the issue of gender violence and intimacy. I draw on feminist and anthropological approaches, discussing the links among intimate partner violence, the engendered subject, and witnessing. Efforts to consider women's testimonies—by legal, social, and law enforcement professionals—pose persistent questions for legal and for anthropological knowledge. In particular, the question of how to conceptually identify consent and subjectivity is made crucial by the elusive entwinement of violence and intimacy. Debates about the amplitude and distinguishing traits of the phenomenon underline the need to reflect on the recognition of facts based on victims' perceptions and statements.

In Chapter Two I show how denouncing violence, pressing charges, and escaping from the perpetrator, have different and contradictory effects on women's persuasiveness according to different institutional requests. Given the specific features of the crime in the Italian law code, the logic of gender violence in public debate fluctuates between the identification of a free, unbound subjectivity and a female, constitutive weakness. The issue of women's responsibility proves crucial in the regime of the indictability of the crime, in the expectations of professionals, and in the court. The meaning of violence, the relevance of the context, and the intimate relationship are what paradoxically make this peculiar 'crime with a story' undetectable.

Chapter Three is about proof and evidence. The intersection of self-reflexivity and vulnerability in testimony highlights how the burden of evidence and the burden of persuasion that constitute proof appear in a relationship of intractable contradiction. The kind of testimonial proof represented by the victim of domestic violence draws on logics of truth that seek to identify her capacity to know and understand her own experience, and to act consequently. Following Foucault's insights about truth and juridical forms, I illustrate how women's plausible testimony is paradoxically elicited in the form of a confession that reproduces an assumed victim-subject.

Chapter Four reflects on intentionality, persuasiveness, and agency. Unexpected testimonies that do not conform to the requirements of authenticity disrupt expectations through peculiar stances and communicative styles. In the face of the hailing of the victim-subject, a figure actually impossible to perform straightforwardly, different ways of telling the truth question the assessment of violence in a productive mockery of legal assumptions about the gendered victim. With these experiments, women eschew the devices that produce the antithetical figures of the manipulative subject to be blamed or the helpless victim to be saved. Unexpected voices and subjectivities of women can provide tools with which to circumvent the impasse in recognizing intimate violence, and to lead astray self-referential and impervious legal devices.

Finally, my concluding remarks reflect on the feminist possibility for the understanding of unexpected subjects through an anthropology of hesitation, profanation, and subtraction.

CHAPTER ONE

(Un)familiar Violence

When we come to a final consideration of the relationship between violence and gender, it is clear that violence of all kinds is engendered in its representation, in the way it is thought about and constituted as a social fact. In its enactment as a social practice, therefore, it is part of a discourse, albeit a contradictory and fragmented discourse, about gender difference.
Henrietta Moore, 1994

The study of violence continues to challenge and channel our disciplinary desires in profound ways.
Veena Das, 2008

Violence Degree Zero

Domestic violence is an awkward and minor object of anthropological research. Too obvious and widespread to constitute a novel issue, it is the quintessential non-exotic subject. A number of studies in various environments—from the legal space and social services to everyday life—have turned the ethnographic gaze towards domestic violence.[1] However, the theme of intimate partner violence remains relatively marginal in the general disciplinary debate and, in particular, in the anthropology of violence.[2] Because of the intercrossing of various fields—psychology, pedagogy, law, and social services—it is rarely chosen for theorization within a disciplinary tradition. Furthermore, domestic violence is a phenomenon that remains largely absent from an emergent ethnography of militancy and civil movements because it identifies anti-heroic subjects: not only are they mostly women, they are also victims. The fact that no geographical space is totally immune from domestic or gendered violence, and that it is a worldwide phenomenon without cultural or national limits, makes the subject less appealing from the anthropological point of view. Given the impossibility of finding class and generational constants, or significant correlations with socio-cultural aspects, domestic violence emerges as a latent element that is found

1. In addition to the edited book by Counts, Brown, and Campbell (1999), and the volume edited by Wies and Haldane (2011), I would cite, among others, Websdale (1998) on rural women in Kentucky; McGilligray and Comaskey (1999) on minorities in Canada; Abraham (2000) on South Asian migrants in the United States; Merry (2000) on colonialism and the law in Hawai'i; McClusky (2001) and Beske (2016) in Belize, Trinch (2003) on Latinas' protection order interviews in the United States, Hautzinger (2007) in Bahia, Brazil; Plesset (2006) on two shelters in Northern Italy; Lazarus-Black (2007) on the legal management of domestic violence in the Caribbean; and Hirsch (1998) on marital disputes in Kenya.
2. A virtual issue of *American Anthropologist* bringing together essays on violence from 1980 to 2012 does not include a single article on this topic (Dominguez 2013). The entry on violence in the *Companion on Moral Anthropology*, edited by Didier Fassin, explicitly leaves out domestic and family violence due to how little it is studied in anthropology (Hinton 2012: 501).

everywhere—albeit in different forms—as a quasi-natural dimension of gender relations. The theme of domestic violence appears paradoxical. Considered too structural to circumscribe, it is both not political enough and at the same time too politicized. Relegated to feminism, as a stand-alone ideology and theory, it represents one of the few cases in which there is a remainder between the relevance of the phenomenon and the theoretical responses provided by the social sciences (Hearn 2012).

Intimate partner violence is one of those "dead zones of the imagination" (Graeber 2012) that eludes critical analysis, not so much because of a lack of relevance but rather because it represents somehow an excess of relevance and deals with fields of common experience that do not lend themselves to a rich and meaningful narrative, therefore representing an authentic disruption of expectations. We may speak of a *violence degree zero*, as a much-debated issue and at the same time an area "of violent simplification" (Graeber 2012: 106). It is a social phenomenon that is globally recognized as evident but also as constitutively submersed. The potential for it to emerge is related to the possibility that victims have of recognizing it and conveying it socially.

These theoretical conundrums in analysis are evident in debates on the evaluation of the magnitude of domestic violence. The general lack of data from several countries is not simply due to the reluctance, idleness, or incapacity of the state or of local institutions to see the phenomenon as relevant. In fact, several obstacles arise when investigating intimate partner violence using quantitative methods, such as the complexity of standardizing elements, including the degree of gravity, and the variables surrounding motive and intentionality. The available statistics are, moreover, often difficult to compare due to their use of different methods and indices.[3] Strikingly, the very issue of intimacy challenges

3. The International Violence Against Women Survey (IVAWS), which uses the same methodology to compare countries,

the definition of a violent act. The complication lies in how victims define violence, and in the influence of the context on the possibility of talking about violence. Victimization surveys may present biases due to the multiple ways that violence can be experienced and described: ethnographic research shows that, instead of abuse and victimization, violence may be read as normal acts of discipline, naturalized as relational gender dynamics. The data relating to recourse to the law are not significant and are even paradoxical: the number of criminal charges and the extent to which violence reaches the surface can even be inversely proportional to its pervasiveness.

Merry and Coutin (2014) have analyzed the deadlock regarding the statistical measurement of social facts and data gathering to meet the need for responses by policy makers. They have emphasized that technologies of knowledge are not at all objective but include cuts, omissions, and selectivity in the definition of phenomena and their relevance. Indices and measuring systems condition the legibility of the phenomena they want to investigate, producing regimes of truth. Discrete and objective unities inevitably obliterate the complexity of events and relations, leading to a flattening of

---

reports that the percentage of European women who have suffered physical or sexual violence at the hands of a current or former partner ranges from 10 percent (Switzerland) to 37 percent (Czech Republic), with Italy reporting 14.3 percent (Johnson et al. 2008). More recent Italian national statistics report that 13.6 percent of women have suffered physical or sexual abuse from a current or former partner, and 26.4 percent have endured psychological violence from their current partner. Only 12.2 percent of women report domestic violence, and only 29.6 percent view it as a crime (Istat 2015). During 2018, Italian newspapers reported 115 cases of femicide: 52 percent of these cases involved violence by a current or former partner; previous violence was reported to authorities only in 9 cases (Casa delle donne per non subire violenza 2018).

experiences, underplaying of contradictions, and the erasure of some facts and highlighting of others. The introduction and problematization of variables such as nationality, religion, ethnicity, gender, sexuality, and class can endanger the possibility of indexing domestic violence:

> [G]lobal surveys require categories that can travel across such cultural borders while remaining commensurable. This situation creates a paradox: the survey categories need to be translated into local terms to measure local ideas and behavior accurately but need to retain their universal meanings to make comparisons possible across these borders. (Merry and Coutin 2014: 6)

The difficulties related to the definition of violence in intimate relations are echoed in the reading of the phenomenon itself: the interpretability of the character of domestic violence is such that there exist divergent positions on its scope and gravity. For instance, the school of family conflict studies suggests that, according to empirical and comparative research, violence in households is generally reciprocal and gender-symmetrical. In this perspective, the gender difference lies in the harsher physical consequences of abuse for women, in the more frequent perception of violence by women, and in more publicity for female as opposed to male victims (Archer 2000; Costa et al. 2015). On the other hand, the violence-against-women approach insists on the unreliability of surveys and research related to such a complex phenomenon, claiming that abused women under-report and normalize intimate violence, and that men assaulted by intimates are more likely to press charges and less willing to drop them. This perspective underlines the necessity of distinguishing between defensive and offensive injuries, as most women who use violence against their partners employ defensive violence in response to ongoing, systematic abuse (Dobash and Dobash 2004; Kimmel 2002). Furthermore, if we accept that women and men suffer intimate partner violence in an identical manner, we must explain the bizarre fact that women who are victims of abuse have been able to construct, although with a lot of difficulty, spaces for discussion, refuges, and help networks, whereas men show—apparently only in this area—a surprising incapacity to channel their own interests into institutions. Does claiming that the perception of violence and its physical consequences is less harsh for men mean that men experience abuse but do not *suffer* from it? In general, the Conflict Tactics Scale methodology, most used in family conflict studies, is marked by the biased assumption that violence is the result of an argument and not the effort to control and prevail, therefore erasing the circumstances and consequences, the nature of the relationship, the motivation and intention for violence, and the gender difference in retrospective estimations of violent acts. These claims of gender symmetry omit a crucial point: the identification and analysis of the dynamics of gender (Kimmel 2002: 1344).

Johnson has explained the differences between the two strands of scholarship, by identifying two distinct phenomena: on the one hand, situational conflict and contestation within the couple, and on the other hand, acts of violence related to domination, or what he calls "intimate terrorism" (Johnson and Leone 2005). The latter implies tactics and strategies of power and control by one partner over the other, which presents specific dynamics that are not captured in the surveys. However, this is a particularly problematic definition, as it identifies a relation in which a subject is at the other's complete disposal, and thus the object of infinite and unlimited violence. Are resistances, strategy, and overthrow not possible in every relation of power? Contestation and domination are very difficult to tackle separately, as are gender relations and power relations. It is therefore the question of the perception of violence—the under- and over-estimation of violence and of victimization by gender—which is problematic in the process of data gathering and in the identification of the social phenomenon. The statistical approach must be objective to the extent to which it requires "little interpretation by the victim" (Merry and Coutin 2014: 6). The emotional consequences of violence—included in the indices on violence against women—pose particular problems for its measurement. This raises questions discussed in feminist theorization and in reflections on violence in anthropology. What is an abusive act? What is violence? To what extent is the victim legitimated or moved to talk about the experience? The anthropological concern about the social use of the term 'violence' produces a paradox: analyzing it means focusing not on the subject who exercises violence (whether institutional, collective, or individual), but on the one who suffers it or witnesses it, who speaks out. An anthropology of violence inevitably tends to focus on the witness and the victim, and on the "political relations between performer and witness" (Riches 1986: 3).

In the last two decades, acknowledgment of the relevance of the social and political dimensions of violence and suffering has led to unprecedented interest in the mutual implications of violence and the production of subjectivity, and to interrogation of the notion of the everyday as the site of the ordinary, in which experience and agency are shaped (Kleinman, Das, and Lock 1997; Das et al. 2000; Biehl, Good, and Kleinman 2007). The movement towards the theorization of interpersonal and structural violence allows shifting attention towards the relationship between subjectivity and power, focusing on the production of the subject as gendered (Moore 2007; Ortner 2006). In this framework, domestic violence emerges as a complex and problematic issue for anthropological reflection. Veena Das, one of those who has most deeply investigated the tangle of violence, intimacy, and subjectivity raises two points that highlight the difficulties in addressing domestic violence. The first refers to the issue of intimacy and emotions: the very notion of intimacy is hardly compatible with a broad definition of violence that even includes harsh language. The second point is the difficulty in conceptually identifying the question of consent (Das 2008: 292-293). These themes are evidently interconnected.

The notion of intimacy is key to reflections on domestic violence and the production of subjectivity. Intimacy and violence in late modern societies are in an apparently contradictory relationship. Love and intimacy have been identified as sites of active trust, where the romantic relationship enables the subject to express him– or herself, so that intimacy between partners is the epitome of modernity (Giddens 1992). In the context of familial abuse, the occurrence of violence brings together love, trust, relationship, desire, and sexuality as exemplary sites of the gendered true self (Rose 1989). The space of intimacy presents a constant tension between ambivalence, ambiguity, and the authentic production of the subject (Sehlikoglu and Zengin 2015). Thus, intimacy shares the duplicity and elusiveness that can be found in the notion of violence. It is a space of scarring experience and, at the same time, a field of irreducibly ambiguous meanings, in some cases even in the perceptions of the subjects involved. The intimacy of past or present couples implies a kind of complicity, sharing, and affection—and forms of trust and dependence that include material conditions of mutual care, the daily sharing of space, shared children, and common plans and money. The vision of an equation between intimacy, reciprocity, solidarity, and trust has been called into question in feminist approaches that have destabilized the assumption of the domestic and reproductive sphere as a safe core. The questions of connection and relatedness, which imply intimacy by definition, have been identified by several scholars as historically associated with sociability, and laden with constitutively positive aspects (Edwards and Strathern 2000; Berlant 2008; Broch-Due and Ystanes 2016). It is no surprise that critiques of Marshall Sahlins' conception of kinship as "mutuality of being" (2013) return the question of gender to the table (Kapila 2013).

In his analysis of the relationship between intimacy and witchcraft, Geschiere suggests that witchcraft might represent the dark side of kinship. Questioning the tenacious vision of kinship and of intimate relationships as spaces of indisputable reciprocity, he emphasizes that addressing intimacy in anthropology means "to follow what people themselves define as intimate—what is 'inside'" (Geschiere 2013: xx). The coalescence between the Latin meanings *intimus* and *vis* in the expression *intimus vis* or "particularly effective violence" (Geschiere 2013: 26) shows that the notion of intimacy can be understood as an attribute of powerful operational violence. Violence can be thought of in relational terms, through the tangle of proximity, relatedness, danger, and intimacy. In this respect, violence may be identified as the dark side of intimacy.

These reflections on violence and intimacy are useful for investigating how law and institutions deal with domestic violence and strive to verify it. The dimension of separation, or rather, of the identification of a personal space not reducible to a shared discourse articulated in abstract terms, marks the experience of intimate violence. This form of immunity, this resistance to knowledge and understanding, is crucial to the anthropological analysis of domestic violence and the ways it is treated by institutions. The victim's intimacy—and her ability to express it as a space in which to investigate, understand, give meaning to, detect, and, finally, prove violence—is decisive precisely in as far as it has to force the limits of the legibility of intimacy in order to become shared. This dark side of intimacy is at the same time *already known* and somehow expected. Vulnerability and violence, and knowledge and discourses about them, are gendered in their very essence.

Gender violence has been theorized and debated for the most part through the particular case of sexual violence. Sexual violence is clearly linked with domestic violence as they share an unequal distribution and heteronormative imbalance of power. The everyday nature of rape has been thematized through various ethnographic works, such as by Bourgois (1995) and by Goldstein (2003). It is a problematic phenomenon to investigate—and not only through ethnographic methodologies—for many of the same reasons that it is hard to investigate domestic violence: its banalization, the difficulty or impossibility of a recourse to law, the dynamics of stigma, the perpetrator's impunity. In her analysis of the encounter of sexually abused women with the institutions in charge of verifying the violent act in the United States, Mulla (2014) has highlighted the processes of revictimization which are operationally and conceptually intertwined with acts of caring for bodies and subjects.

Violence in intimate relations enters into the daily, domesticated, normal dynamics of gender relations, beyond the state of exceptionality. It is a violence of the most personal sort, one-on-one, often committed in the most private context (the home), by the most intimate person (the partner). Despite the well-known circuit of social and family violence exerted on victims, the social dimension might be legally irrelevant. Domestic violence is never a group phenomenon, involving as it does a single perpetrator and a single victim, with the victim and perpetrator bound in a relationship of intimacy, emotion, and living together, with predictable ambivalence. External witnesses are sporadic at best and often, except for children, no one else is familiar with the facts of the case, or is willing to speak. Intimate partner violence is often an open secret, sometimes accepted and generally overlooked by those who are close to the couple: friends, relatives, neighbors. The intervention of institutions is seen as risky, the intimate and the domestic are viewed as spheres that must be protected from state intervention, so as to avoid unwanted and uncontrolled outcomes. Due to the intimacy-related implications, public exposure of a violent relationship may be tantamount to an admission of incapacity in choosing a partner, and the failure of a life project. In rape cases, the woman's reaction is taken to signify her having suffered an act of violence, not her having participated in an act of mutual aggression. The fact that violence may be—and frequently is—reciprocated through some kind of action unquestionably complicates cases of domestic violence beyond even those of rape. In cases of domestic violence, the dimension of time (which defines the crime itself, as continued misconduct), and difficulties in the certification of injuries in sequence, make the collection of bodily evidence (Mulla 2014) less crucial. Consequently, the agency, experience and perception of the victim, in intimate relationship with the perpetrator, draw the boundaries of the phenomenon.

Mistreated Subjects and Intractable Violence

The relation between gender and violence in anthropological terms has identified the historical relationship of tension between feminism and anthropology, indicated by Strathern (1987), as a privileged space to rethink ethnographic knowledge (Harvey and Gow 1994). What kind of commitment is possible, and how can the experience of violence be addressed, given that "the objectification and disassociation involved in the politics of naming and revealing requires the imposition of absolute values on particular practices regardless of how these are understood by those involved" (Harvey and Gow 1994: 5). The connection between anthropological analysis and feminist stances becomes decisive in the production of a critical dynamic that constantly questions the efficacy of a political practice. Here, the politics of naming violence is decisive. Indeed, the critique of abstract notions of subjectivity, and the complex knot that links violence to subjection, witnessing, and agency, are crucial both in feminist theory and in anthropological work addressing gender (Butler 1997a; Das 2007; Spivak 1988). The relation between experience and the subject has become the focus of reflections on gender, violence, and dominance in a critique of modernist feminist generalizations from the experiences of western, heterosexual, white, middle-class women (Abu-Lughod 2002; hooks 1984; Mohanty 1984). If in "having a voice" and "claiming one's voice" politics and epistemology converge, nonetheless, the transparency of voice as an expression of subjective experience, in the conflation of knowledge and consciousness, is constantly put to the test by ethnography (Keane 2000: 271).

A much-debated issue in critical theory, and an antinomic, nonlinear, and slippery object, violence raises fundamental questions for anthropology. The contested meaning of the term itself demonstrates the problem of defining it as a discrete phenomenon, and points towards its qualitative character. The invisibility and legitimation of different forms of violence are related to the gradation and magnitude of its limits and excesses beyond a socially acceptable and 'normal' level of violence. David Graeber calls into question the differences between structural violence and structures of violence, in an admission of the oblivion and (re)discovery of the relevance of feminist reflection:

> [R]acism, sexism, poverty, these cannot exist except in an environment defined by the ultimate threat of actual physical force. To insist on a distinction only makes sense if one wishes, for some reason, to also insist that there *could* be, for example, a system of patriarchy that operated in the total absence of domestic violence, or sexual assault—despite the fact that, to my knowledge, no such system has ever been observed." (Graeber 2012: 113)

Regarding the question of the definition of structural violence and symbolic violence, the materialist feminist tradition has pointed out that identifying a violence exerted through the diffuse perception of the legitimacy of power, without the need to resort to force, eclipses the relevance of the threat of the exercise of force (Mathieu 1999). Yet the potential for the use of physical force does not resolve the conundrums related to the subject and to forms of subjection, or rather, the essential connection among the manifestation of truth, the government of individuals, and the constitution of subjectivity, resistance, and agency that feminist reflection constantly interrogates.

The dimension of the judicial institution allows us to further investigate the potential of the exercise of violence. How can the threat or the fear of violence be considered within an apparatus of law created to verify such violence? In his analysis of asylum courts in the United Kingdom, Anthony Good (2007: 53) remarks upon the rejection of subjective elements, such as fear, in favor of the objective situation: that of which one could reasonably be afraid. Including the subjective dimensions of witnesses into the picture would mean rewarding cowards and penalizing the brave, and furthermore failing to consider the cultural components in the production and expression of feelings. To elicit violence and allow it to be identified as such, it is necessary to abandon subjective meaning in favor of common sense. Yet the meaning of violence for the abused subject is crucial. Violence and gender are implicated in forms of subjectivity: the subject is constructed through dominant models of discourse and practice that produce and reproduce the notions of individuality and agency. To address the meaning given to violence by the victim does not mean to undervalue the acts of violence; on the contrary, it means understanding the peculiarity of intimate violence, the issue of dominance and power, and the "countercurrents of subjectivity" (Ortner 2006: 126). Reflections on intimate violence and the law precisely must investigate the boundary between subject and power, the constitutive remainder between these two dimensions. The victim's experience and consciousness, the possibility for her to speak in her own voice, and the effectiveness of this speech as a speech act, all prove crucial in the legal testimony of domestic violence.

The legal treatment of women revolves around paradox (Hirsch and Lazarus-Black 1994). Law questions and subordinates by categorizing, while at the same time it produces forms of empowerment. Through stabilizing borders, it is by definition classificatory. It is precisely in this way that it produces sentences, traces spaces of legality, and is exposed to change. Law both reflects and forges relations of power, molding subjectivities at the same time as it molds discourse, codes, communication, processes, and power (Hirsch and Lazarus-Black 1994: 17). Feminist critiques have debated the notion of subjectivity, revealing the liberal order as a historical product, and problematizing the exclusively negative conceptualization of liberty according to which agency carries liberal visions of autonomy, control, and individual action, possession, and commodification. Feminist jurisprudence in its different versions not only considers the formal and *de facto* constraints that impede women's access to a state of individual autonomy, it also calls into question the features of the concept of autonomy as they have become consolidated in liberal thought and its application. The issues of consent, experience, and the dimension of corporeality, are privileged spaces for reflection on the gendered subject and the law. Sexual offences have a particular ability to reveal the problematics of law and the sort of "moral magic" that consent entails (Cowan 2007: 66).

The feminine emerges as an unforeseen element in the legal field, the dimension that calls into question the binary logics of truth–untruth, guilt–innocence, and consent–nonconsent (Minow 1990; Pateman 1988; Smart 1989). The law's claim to truth in rape trials unavoidably frames an alternative: consent is to be presumed whenever the lack of it is not established, leaving out considerations such as the constraints inherent in various degrees of intimacy, submission, and fear of violence. This is a vision that assumes a notion of free consent in a state of nature, not marked by historical and social dynamics, in which coercion and consent are general, logical axioms that precede sexuality (Butler 1997b: 95). How can we consider an illocution that does not respond to the requirement of being taken up by the interlocutor, and is therefore not 'fully' successful? As Fricker (2007: 140-141) says, "In sexual contexts at least, a woman's 'No' does not receive its required uptake from a man, with the result that her would-be illocution thereby fails to communicate—it fails even to *be* the illocutionary act it would have been." Nonetheless, it remains more than noise, haunting legal reasoning. When domestic violence includes sexual violence, further difficulties emerge in understanding what is meant by forced sex. Shonna Trinch (2003) has remarked the blurred boundaries of intimate violence, in her work on the linguistic and cultural translation from oral story to written report in protective order applications in rape cases by intimate partners among Latina women in the United States.

The complexity of defining and taking account of domestic violence that is found in debates in the social sciences can also be traced in the legal dimension. Law is a crucial site in the investigation of the victim's subjectivity, consent, and agency in cases of domestic violence, as it is a space where the perception and the verification of the violent event meet. An ethnography of the legal treatment of domestic violence allows one to delve into this investigative work. The subjective dimension of domestic violence attributes a specific weight to the speech of the victim, implying a particular focus on her responsibility in speaking out. The requirement by the law and institutions that she must speak about violence identifies a subjectivity that expresses itself through its experience and demand for justice. The definition of the battered woman is linked to the fact of having suffered a certain condition over time and not having talked about it, of being a silenced victim (Hirsch 1998: 290). Therefore, being able to tell one's story in the courtroom, and assuming an authoritative voice, requires somehow a mutation in one's condition. In the framework of the crime of family abuse, the act of talking contradicts the victim's inability to speak that is the underlying assumption of the legal process. By definition, the woman who has suffered violence cannot speak. Her voice is not authoritative but, precisely because she is subjected to social pressures that silence her, she is called on by the state to talk about her condition. The space of the legal process in itself becomes the ritual space in which her subjectivity has the chance to change its sign. It opens up the possibility of speaking differently than expected.

In the pursuit of evidence in trials of domestic violence that focus on the demonstration of continued misconduct, it is not the violent act that is subjected to scrutiny but rather the testimony itself and, by extension, the woman, the subject, her relationship with her partner, her suffering—in a nutshell, her life experience. If right is the form that the relation takes in a commodity economy (Strathern 1999; Viveiros de Castro and Fausto 2017: 59), the interpellation of claiming rights is a form of political demand that abused women take responsibility for themselves, taking an oath that is at once ethical (feminist self-awareness) and aesthetic (being adequate and workable within the legal frame). Interpretations of law deriving from theories of sexual difference tend to identify the ethical with the feminine, and to cast women's experiences and words as escaping representation in language, as that which lies beyond violent or difference-repressing institutionalization. In so doing, they place "an undue theoretical burden on the concept of sexual difference," attributing to "the *feminine* a set of associations or responsibilities which bear a striking resemblance to those imposed on *woman* in nineteenth and early twentieth-century anti-feminist or separatist discourse" (Lacey 2002: 120).

In his political and institutional ethnology of truth-speaking, Foucault addresses how subjects are actually implicated in forms of veridiction. In proposing an analysis of modes of veridiction rather than an epistemology of truth, a description of technologies of subjectivation rather than a deduction of the Subject, Foucault deploys an ontology of discourses of truth. At the center of his reflection there is a genealogy of truth-telling (*le dire vrai*) and of how forms of veridiction generate specific forms of subjection and subjectivation (2014). Here, between power (normativity) and knowledge (intelligibility), Foucault focuses on the notion of the subject and particularly the ways subjects understand and form themselves as subjects of experiences. The emphasis on who labels a given act as violent, in a context in which the only witness is the victim, takes us to the center of reflections on talking about violence, denouncing it and making it evident, expressing one's own experience, and at the same time bringing it to the attention of the law. The procedures of the individualization of the victimized female subject, and the interpellation to speak out and against, create a space in which intimate violence can be rethought and recognized institutionally, beginning from the testimony.

It is well-known that the relationship of Foucault with feminism is particularly problematic. Despite his support for feminist campaigns, such as those regarding abortion rights, he nonetheless did not consider feminism as a critical and intellectual reference. His reflections on sexual violence in particular have been a field of overt dissent by feminist thinkers. In a 1977 collective conversation on the issue of repression, when questioned on rape prosecution, Foucault expressed how it posed a dilemma—later described as embarrassing, discomfiting (2014: 263)—to his stance regarding the need to subtract sexuality, and everything that has to do with sexuality, from law making. He therefore proposed to consider sex as any other part of the body (a hand, a hair), and rape as every other physical aggression, like a punch in the face (Foucault 2001: 351-353). In a prompt reply, Plaza clarifies that the peculiarity of sexual violence lies in the eminently social dimension of sexuality and gender. Defining women as social class (which also comprises men when they are sexually abused, as they are socially feminized by a sexually violent act), she traces back normative heterosexuality "to a position close to rape" (Plaza [1978] 1981: 33). If feminism claims that the sexual organ might become considered as any other part of the body, it is not possible to behave as if it already is: "It is certainly not we who wish that the sexual organ not be a hair: *it is exactly this that we are demanding*. But we cannot function in an ideal state and act as if —here and now— the sexual organ was a hair!" (Plaza 1981: 32; emphasis in original). This sentence underlines how feminist issues are, in an anthropologically relevant way, rooted in time and space. There is an unsolved tension between the chance to rethink and free gender differences, to diffract them on the one hand, and the embodied realities, the experiential dimension, on the other. Sex is not *yet* something else. It could be something else, but it is not: as a matter of fact, the experience of sexual violence is not comparable to a punch in the face. The issue of experience, and the possibility of conveying it, are therefore relevant to any consideration of the intricacies of intimacy, violence, and testimony.

Feminist post-structuralist theory has been influenced by the Foucauldian insight that experience is understood as the correlation between fields of knowledge, types of normativity, and forms of subjectivity, putting forward a radically de-subjectified vision of experience in which there is no space for a "foundational 'female experience' grounded in the communalities of women's embodiment" (Oksala 2004: 101). This perspective considers experience not as incontestable evidence that can emerge once it has been made visible, but rather as a process through which subjectivity is produced. It contests the notion of the "communication of knowledge gained through (visual, visceral) experience" (Scott 1991: 776). Yet, this stance did not mean to dismiss the issue of truth and the pursuit of justice. The tension between women's rights and post-structuralist feminism poses the problem of constantly making up the language of rights in order to eschew the set-back of a universal language that conceals power relationships, and to escape the impasse of its liberal premises. Drawing on Spivak, Brown acknowledges that rights are what "we cannot not want," while stressing how women's rights might "build a fence," hypostatizing the feminine as trans-historically subordinate (2000: 232). The paradox she reveals is "that rights that entail some specification of our suffering, injury or inequality lock us into the identity defined by our subordination, while rights that eschew this specificity not only sustain the invisibility of our subordination, but potentially even enhance it" (Brown 2000: 232).

The practices and diverse ways of eliciting narratives of violence, and women's autobiographical accounts, have been largely debated in feminist circles, where positions that claim the possibility and necessity of women's speaking for themselves are counter-posed to those that highlight the mystification of referring to a humanist, feminist subject. The "either/or debate about truth telling" (Valverde 2004: 67) has radicalized positions, flattening a nuanced issue. If the debate on experience has made it a much more complex and elusive category, truth telling is still integral to ethical and feminist reflections. Valverde has shown that truth telling can be produced through modes that do not necessarily imply an inner psychic self of humanistic legacy, but more pragmatic and flexible figures of ethical selfhood.

Ethnography can respond to the call to pursue a different path, beyond this impasse, by trying to identify possibilities opened daily within the institutional framework in which facts must be verified. The tangled issue of experiences of domestic violence lies at the intersection of intimacy, violence, and the subject, eschewing an image of the feminine as an essentialized subject who occupies a position of complete exteriority in relation to the law. At the same time, this twine allows us to insist on the issue of truth, a truth that is unsayable within the juridical canon and that constantly questions it. In cases of domestic violence (and sexual assault), it is so difficult to define the evidence of the 'fact' because the fact itself is defined a posteriori, since its very existence depends on how it is interpreted as experience. A posteriori knowledge is not necessary or universal: it is knowledge of something that is proven through experience, rather than derived from an abstract truth. Was the act perceived as violence? Was there consent? Was there some kind of provocation? These questions in turn entail the notion of limit: up to what point? As much as the field of domestic violence may overlap with that of sexual violence, domestic violence involves more difficulties in establishing the facts. In intimate partner violence, the court investigates the limits by evaluating the intimate relationship the victim maintained with the perpetrator over time: to what extent was it simply a conflictual relationship?

The institutional form has been identified, in Italy and elsewhere, as a space that is hardly capable of taking gender violence into consideration in all its complexity. Social services and the juridical system, in their claimed neutrality and thus self-referentiality, are revealed as institutions that do not recognize the particular nature of intimate partner violence. In this framework, feminist and anthropological explorations have problematized the rhetoric of the value of taking a position against violence using one's own authentic voice, seeing silences as a method for questioning institutions' objectivity and knowledge (Charlesworth 1999; Cabot 2016). In the process of authentication, law constantly restores the figure of the statement, ascribing to the speaking subject what has been said in the process of connecting enunciations—as the intentional agentive subject of modern jurisprudence is answerable for its acts and for potentially infinite relations and wrongs (Pottage 2014: 153). This mechanism becomes decisive in the context of the centrality of the victim's voice in the legal processes regarding domestic violence, and the consequent back-seat granted to the perpetrator, who is not called upon to speak but must be revealed through the work of the court. In the experience of violence, the intimacy and intentionality on which liability is based become the primary spaces for the demonstration of criminal action. The liability of the accused is highlighted by the Italian expression *imputato*, the person to whom a potential responsibility is ascribed, attributed, and assigned. The victim who testifies is called a *teste*, witness, as is every other figure who testifies in the trial. Yet the intentionality of the perpetrator in using violence is given little consideration in comparison to the intentionality of the woman to speak of violence, to witness her experience.

The ethnographic reflection that I propose here traces the internal logic of juridical processes that identify the voice and the subjectivity of those who have suffered violence, pinpointing a specific form of judgment at play between the autonomy of the facts and contextualization. Here, the process of getting to know the witness's intentions and dispositions is crucial. The woman victim is in fact not only *testis* (the third party), but also *superstes* (survivor, as in Fassin 2008). She testifies on the basis of her experience, not on observation, because she has lived through the events. The characteristic of the violent act is that, in order to be recognized, it has to be perceived as such by the person who suffers it. The *Italian Encyclopedia of Law* explains the difference between *vis* and *violentia*: *vis* refers to the agent only, whereas *violentia* involves both the act of the agent and the consequences for the subject. *Violentia dicitur ex parte patientis*: the act can be defined as violent only by those who suffered (Calasso 1958: 844).

In the next chapter, I will address the subjectivity of the abused victim, and the articulation between silence, words, and hesitation in the institutional contexts related to domestic violence, starting from the Italian case. I focus on the different demands that interpellate the abused subject, and on what happens when the law addresses intimate violence through eliciting the whole intimate history of abuse as the meaningful context. Intimacy is not only what is on stage and has to be investigated, and as such requires a story. It is also something that has to do with the ways the law acknowledges the gendered subject as victim.

CHAPTER TWO

Wavering Intentions

Along with the history of resistances we need a history of hesitations.
James Clifford, 1988

To be a woman is to be in a situation.
Judith Butler, 2016

Recognize and Speak the Violence!

Walking into the courthouse room, I sit down next to the plaintiff. Carla[1] is a woman in her early forties. I met her a few months earlier, during a postponement of the hearing. She is not the one who pressed charges against the man who abused her—her neighbors, to whom she had run to escape the violence, did so—and therefore the lawyer for the prosecution is not present. She looks very tense. A woman lawyer, who I realize only later is with the defense, rather than the prosecution, comes over to reassure her, saying: "You just have to tell us what happened." The woman judge has been persuaded by the defense to begin the day's docket with this trial for familial abuse and personal injury, as Carla has to return in a few hours to the battered women's shelter where she has been living for the last three years. The

1. All personal names are pseudonyms.

judge calls on her to testify. Carla's posture is aloof, and she answers questions in a near whisper, often in monosyllables, constantly staring straight ahead of her like an automaton. At times she appears completely disengaged, failing to answer questions and remaining motionless. Her expression is extremely serious, and she does not show any fear, pain, or anger. She narrates the events of her abuse with an air of detachment, even stating only quickly that she was pregnant at the time, as if it were irrelevant. The judge and the public prosecutor look at each other in discomfort. The events had taken place four years earlier:

Public Prosecutor: What did he do when you locked yourself in the bathroom?
Carla: He knocked on the door.
PP: In what way? Did he try to open it?
C: Yes.
PP: Here it is written: "He tried to break it down." Do you confirm this?
C: Yes.
PP: And then what?
C: I didn't know what to do, confront him or run away through the balcony. I escaped through the balcony, using the water pipe.
PP: How high up was the balcony?
C: I don't know… four meters… I don't know…
PP: So? Did you fall?
C: I slid down and started to run, I asked for help at the neighbors. And I hurt my arm sliding down. The police came and they took me to the emergencies, I was three months pregnant.
[…]
PP: The previous incident discussed earlier, was it the only time prior to this one?
C: [*Silence*] Yes. [*Looks off into space*]
PP: Can you provide more details? Do people usually go to the police for a little familial quarrel?

C: [*Silence*]
Judge: Was there more? Against you?
C: Against me. He grabbed me by the throat. But only by the throat, that's it.
J: Did he shove you?
C: No.
PP: Did your partner use to drink?
C: He used to drink sometimes. Not always.
PP: Away from home?
C: Yes.
PP: And would he show violent behavior when he came back home?
C: Yes.
PP: You declared that this was only the second time, now you're saying something else. That he used to drink and showed violent behavior.
C: [*Silence*]
J: Do you understand what the prosecutor is saying? That you said before that only two violent events occurred, but now you are saying there were others.
C: No, only those two episodes.
J: Has he ever acted aggressively?
C: No.[2]

What does this numb and evasive testimony—with no pauses, language, or facial expressions to emphasize events that might be considered important—tell us? What expectations of legal professionals for victims' courtroom testimony does it fail to meet? The Italian legal system is set up in a way that fosters an interrogation of the status of intimate partner violence as evidence, together with the fundamental concepts of fact, truth, and justice. Trials for *maltrattamenti in famiglia* (familial abuse) grant pride of place to the victim's testimony, which can stand alone in incriminating the defendant, and can constitute the basis

2. Field notes, February 20, 2011.

for a conviction. As it is up to the victim to prove domestic violence, she is granted a central place in the trial. Because in the majority of cases the accused chooses not to appear in court and exercises his right not to speak (*contumace*, in Italian), the plaintiff's testimony ends up playing a pivotal role in hearings. Officials I interviewed underlined the decisive role that is played by the victim's testimony. As a criminal court judge said:

> The plaintiff's testimony can be sufficient for conviction, but it must be rigorously examined from an 'intrinsic' perspective, for the coherence, precision, composure and objectivity with which the facts are brought to light, and from an 'extrinsic' point of view, ensuring that there is nothing that undermines the reliability of the person.[3]

Article 572 of the Criminal Code dedicated to partner violence, *Maltrattamenti contro familiari e conviventi* (Abuse of family members and live-in partners), derives from the fascist-era Rocco Code.[4] The crime entails mandatory prosecution (*procedibilità di ufficio*) so that the trial goes ahead even if the woman retracts her statement. Furthermore, it calls for clear evidence that the violent acts in question were repeated over time (*abitualità della condotta* or continued

3. Interview with female penal judge. Office of Criminal Court, Bologna, March 2011.
4. In the previous code of 1889, partner violence fell under crimes against another person, while in the Rocco code that replaced it in 1930 it is included under "crimes against the family" and specifically the category of "crimes against familial assistance." It refers to two different types of behavior in that it punishes those "who abuse a family member," that is to say, a member of the nuclear family, or those who abuse an individual in a position of physical or psychological inferiority: a minor below the age of fourteen, a person under their authority or who has been entrusted to them for education, instruction, care, safekeeping, or custody.

conduct). If these crimes have not been committed on a regular basis, then they are referred to different articles of the code, in general judged to be less serious and with more lenient penalties.[5] Evidence thus relies on narrating the experience of violence: the court considers events that took place over time, and evaluates the victim's relationship with the perpetrator. In the hearings of domestic violence that I observed, the public prosecutor and judge were often noticeably irritated by the witness's constant contradictions or memory lapses, and became impatient when she was unable to provide a clear, incontrovertible, and plausible account, or to focus on a specific episode without drifting into another, highlighting events that were irrelevant from a legal point of view. Often the victim's testimony appeared as suspended in its capacity to assert. In some cases, women did not wish to participate actively in the trial.

The victim's position in the trial is thus ambiguous because the mandatory prosecution rule means that she might be called on to participate in the trial against her will. For different reasons, which are related to economic, practical, and sentimental issues, she may decide not to proceed or may

---

5. Intimate partner violence in Italy is very often fragmented into different crimes (personal injury, private violence, threat, insult) rather than classified as the crime of *maltrattamenti in famiglia*. Nearly all the cases for these lesser crimes end up being heard by a small claims judge (*Giudice di Pace*), whose normal job is to bring about conciliation. The Italian penal system establishes two different criminal courts depending on the seriousness of the crime: in the collegial system, the judge is accompanied by two additional judges and, usually, by the court clerk. Apart from a case that was about attempted homicide, I was present in monocratic court hearings that involved a single judge accompanied by a court clerk. In addition to the judge and clerk, the other institutional actors involved in the hearing included the public prosecutor, a lawyer for the defendant, and another for the plaintiff, when required.

end up having second thoughts and dropping the charges. Her intimate relationship, her children with the perpetrator, and the fear of possible consequences in terms of custody, can play equally important roles. Most of the women whom I interviewed at the shelter did not press charges and did not begin a legal process. The difficulty of dealing with crimes of abuse in the family is linked to the retraction of allegations. In addition, these retractions are more complex than those concerning other crimes, precisely because they involve relationships, the family, and affection. In Italy, the percentage of retractions of statements regarding crimes linked to intimate violence is, in fact, very high.[6]

Generally speaking, the law tends to be at odds with questions of intimacy, and the entrance of the law into the intimate sphere implies the contamination of the private space, which is by definition outside of public scrutiny. The government of space through the restraining order (Merry 2001), and of time through multiple appointments with the judicial system over several years, help to contain the violence but can also be a potential impetus for the perpetrator to break the imposed limits.[7] Hence, those who work in shelters, beyond the crucial instrument of the restraining order, are called upon to welcome each woman's decision as to whether or not they will press charges, to guarantee their safety, and to work for the endurance of the charge in order to give victims the support required. According to judges I interviewed, the retraction of allegations—even

6. In Bologna, 61 percent of charges are withdrawn during the investigative or trial phase (Arcidiacono and Crocitti 2015).
7. In Italy, during 2010-2014, 68 percent of female homicides had been committed by the partner. In 44 percent of the cases, the reason for the crime is the end of the relationship; the three months following separation are the most dangerous, when more than half of the femicides occur. Ten per cent of the women killed by a partner or ex-partner had pressed charges (Eures 2015).

though it should have no effect on the development of the trial—in fact creates a context in which the demonstration of violence becomes particularly difficult. As one public prosecutor explicitly stated, retracting the allegations can compromise the outcome of the trial:

> In theory, the retraction of allegations of familial abuse should not have any effect whatsoever. This is in theory. The reality is different, because if I have an aggrieved party who is the only witness and is non-collaborative, the trial is already over. Because it's true that I have to go ahead *ex officio*, but I must also carry out a trial in which the aggrieved person goes in front of a judge and repeats things that they said in their statement. If they don't do that, or they only do it partially, or in a recalcitrant way or something, the trial is destined to fail. So, it's true that I have to proceed regardless, but it's also true that it will never obtain a conviction; these are two truths [*smiles*].[8]

Furthermore, the magistrates are aware that focusing on the reasons for retraction is double-edged: if they try to reveal possible pressure by the violent partner, they might have to accuse him of extortion, which means that the victim is potentially liable for suppressing evidence and false testimony.

The theme of pressing charges is one of the most complicated parts of victims' narratives and is related to different choices, judgments, and behaviors. While describing to me her difficulties with the legal process, a young woman claimed that the law should take priority over the choices of the victim. If the law works, it is only because it is delinked from any of the victim's decisions: "the police force should set the whole process going, even when he has

8. Interview with female public prosecutor, Office of Procura, Bologna, June 2011.

only hit you once. It needs to reach trial even if the woman says no."[9] However, if the law knows, acts, and speaks for the victim, and goes ahead mandatorily, it is destined to fail. The same woman admitted that the trial of her case failed despite the fact that a police supervisor insisted that she take it to court: "He managed to make them take it to trial. Although I said 'No, I don't want to charge him, no, I don't want a trial,' he managed to get it to trial. But then at the trial the judge acquitted him because I didn't testify." In other legal contexts, in particular those of common law, when faced with doubts and reluctance by abused women, it is possible to proceed to trial without hearing the victim's testimony. In contrast, in Italy, the testimony is central, even in cases where the charge has been retracted. The following passage from a hearing illustrates precisely this point. The witness, who I sat next to, expressed her displeasure with comments and gestures during her children's testimony, which exonerated the father and ex-partner. However, once called by the judge to testify, she expressed hesitation and forgiveness, making reference to her feelings. Not wanting to proceed, she retracted her statement:

Defense: Why, on day X, did you drop the charges?
Witness: It was all over.
D: What do you mean by that?
W: It was all over. Because the court was no longer of any use…
[...]
D: Did your husband beat you?
W: No, no. Slaps sometimes, shoves, some hard slaps, but never beaten in a violent way, never…
[...]
Judge: How often did your husband beat the children?
W: Not very often, he's not a drunkard or someone who has strange and bad habits. He is a strong person,

9. Interview with Paola, Casa delle donne, Bologna, July 2010.

determined. We also argued, due to jealousy… we were in love… [*Smiles*]
J: Once a week?
W: [*Evasive*] Me too sometimes, I slapped the children a few times.[10]

Revictimization during trials is generally acknowledged by the victim, the legal team, social workers, police force, and the lawyers of the women's shelter. That which Garapon (1997) attributes to the accused in his archaeology of the judicial setting of civil law—the conditions of alienation, inferiority, and disorientation, the expectations to adhere to the courtroom rules, the fundamental impossibility of using words which have enough weight—is in these cases borne by the victim, who is not legally required to have a defense.

The issue of respecting silences is a problematic element, often discussed in debates at the women's shelter in Bologna that focused on the impossibility of speaking and the choice of not talking, at least not in a public and legal setting. There was also much discussion of how workers in the shelter could manage their frustration when faced with a subject who drops charges, does not return to the shelter, does not answer the telephone, and, in short, disappears. The encouragement to talk takes place in protected spaces, where women are invited to share their experiences with the shelter workers and with other women who find themselves in similar situations. In case they decide to press charges, lawyers working at the shelter are available to assist them. Conversely, despite it not being technically necessary, social services managers take the legal route for granted as a substantial requirement if one wants to proceed with service use, to the extent to which the legal process certifies violence for institutions and at the same time represents a woman's taking responsibility. This insistence arises precisely from women's ambivalence regarding their companions.

10. Field notes, October 18, 2010.

As a social worker maintained, "they press charges, then withdraw them, they kick them out, then let them move back in, it is very complicated."[11] Social workers do not ask to be persuaded, but they do ask women to guarantee that they will not disappear, that they will stick to a certain conduct and be worthy of the services given. Consequently, this ambivalence is reproduced by the demands that institutions place on female victims of violence when pressing charges, demands that simultaneously generate two contradictory messages: on the one hand, social service professionals ask women to press charges *no matter what*, in order to access services; on the other hand, the justice system expects that the charges are not only a means to an end and that the women be fully committed to the sentencing process. The practice of pressing charges instrumentally, as a precautionary and useful tool, is viewed as omissive. Indeed, the importance given to pressing charges, as an act undertaken volitionally by women, is accompanied at the same time by the perception that victims often take this step simply to protect themselves or to warn their partners.

During interviews, legal and social work professionals constantly stressed how the plaintiff must be encouraged to be clear with herself. This perceived lack of determination and clarity in the statements and stances of women who have suffered violence from intimate partners is known in the literature. Professionals express this frustration by posing the infamous Freudian, ultimately unanswered question: "What do women want?" Victims of domestic violence appear too difficult or uncooperative, and "there is no way to tell" what victims really want (Mills 2003: 48). In the Italian context, it is the act of filing charges that makes the woman a conscious victim, one reliable enough to take legal action. *Denunciare* (pressing charges) means taking the floor as a legal subject in order to demand justice, but it also implies speaking out, exposing oneself publicly,

11. Interview with social worker, Bologna, June 2011.

and making the matter explicit; in other words, taking a stance. As Bourdieu (1982) notes, following Benveniste, words related to law in Indo-European languages have their roots in the verb 'to speak' because enacting the law involves performative utterances concerning the power of the institution that grants authority to these utterances. The theme of recounting violence, of speaking out and pressing charges, appears constantly in domestic abuse trials as women are urged to recognize and name the guilty party. This message is also conveyed through recent campaigns against gender violence in Italy. Unlike in the Anglo-American world, in Italy, campaigns concerning violence against women are still in their beginnings, only recently launched in response to the findings of the first national statistical survey in 2008. For instance, the 2013 national campaign *Riconosci la violenza* (Recognize violence) showed the picture of a man's face covered by the slogan: "Violence comes in many forms. Learn how to recognize them. A violent man does not deserve your love. He deserves a charge."[12] In this respect, speaking about violence becomes tantamount to pressing charges; that is, the act of naming violence carried out by a subject is constituted by normative notions of agency. Indicating the perpetrator, speaking out, and acting by leaving the violent partner: all these elements converge in a pedagogical aim.

The actions of professionals are aimed at supporting the subject in her determination to proceed with legal action, acknowledging her hesitation, ascertaining if she is strong enough to maintain the charges, and eliciting the whole story. This emerges from the words of a law enforcement superintendent who explained the difficulties of intervention in cases of domestic violence, and the need to create a climate of mutual trust: "They don't want to tell [the story]. And how can we plan our intervention without

12. http://www.riconoscilaviolenza.it/

a story?"[13] In order to perform the meaning of pressing charges, namely a request for judgment, women have to tell all: about the violence and about their relationship with the perpetrator. During my interviews, social workers shared the view that it is crucial for women to speak out by pressing charges. As a social services manager explained, the road from the charges onward is particularly rough and humiliating, and it entails the ability to "run the gauntlet." However, despite this awareness of the problematic nature of pressing charges, professionals reluctantly admit that this one step makes a huge difference in the way social services take on a specific case, affecting as it does the degree of credibility attributed to the victim of abuse:

> After pressing charges, the path from there on is very complex: the interrogations, to verify if it is true or false, if we have done all the necessary, [if] she went to the emergencies, and if she got it certified or not. So often, the things we give these women in return punish them instead of helping them. [...] We believe them more if they have pressed charges [*sighs*] because they have done something difficult, that is, acted, which is not instinctive. It is somehow less instinctive than simply saying "he has hit me" or "he hits me."[14]

Social workers must express a judgment about the woman, helping to sanction the veracity of her statements, taking a position on the facts and the truth of what she says, so as to allow the law to ratify them. It is not surprising that one woman identified the social services as "the arm of the judge outside of the courtroom." Speaking to institutions about the violence that she suffered at the hands of her partner meant forcing her personal biography into a pre-existent moral code.

13. Interview with superintendent of the Carabinieri station. Metropolitan Bologna area, March 2011.
14. Interview with social service manager, Bologna, July 2011.

This code, and the victim's subjectivity that is required, are tightly linked to the crime of familial abuse. The debated ways in which crimes against women are described in the penal code reflect the contradictions between the necessity of giving a woman the option not to press charges, the need to do so in order to be taken care of by social services, and the image of a victim in need of protection against a hostile context and against her very own choices, despite her having to hold the final responsibility for her decisions.

Maltrattamenti in Famiglia and the Abused Subject

Feminist struggles and debates in Italy have mainly succeeded in impacting legal practices with regard to sexual violence, significantly reshaping the definition of the crime and how it is managed in the courtroom. The first judgment in Italy involving the prosecutability of rape between spouses was handed down in 1976. Only since 1996 has rape no longer been classified as a crime against morality but rather as a crime against the person.[15] Over time there have indeed been courageous stances, such as that of the Sicilian seventeen-year-old Franca Viola who in 1965 refused a shotgun marriage, after being kidnapped and raped by a rejected ex-fiancé, and pressed charges against him, becoming an icon for women's struggles that would shortly thereafter spread

15. A proposal to reform the law through a citizens' initiative dates back to 1979. It emerged from a political climate of feminist struggles over abortion and divorce, and the wide resonance of the 1974 "Circeo murder" in which one young woman lost her life and another managed to escape by pretending to be dead. The violence was committed by a group of three men from the "good side" of Rome, none of whom had a criminal record. It was only in 1996 that a new law eliminated norms regarding seduction as a promise of marriage, kidnapping for reasons of lust, and the protection of the honor of women and the family.

across the country. The issue of rape and justice became widely known through the broadcast of a rape trial in 1979 by the RAI (Italian state television company) that opened up public debate, demonstrating the culture of focusing on the victim's morality and showing the pornographic voyeurism of the court in relation to the witness statement. In this trial for the rape of an eighteen-year-old, the modalities of exposure of the victim, and the general management of the proceedings, led Tina Lagostena Bassi, the lawyer of the civil party, to formulate a now-renowned plea, questioning the court by insisting on women's freedom:

> Because the defense is sacrosanct, inviolable, it is true. But no one of us, lawyers, would ever think of setting up a defense for a robbery the same way a defense for sexual violence is set up. [...] And this is a routine: the woman is on trial. [...] I do not want to talk about Fiorella, I believe that it is humiliating for a woman to come here and stress that she is not a whore. A woman has the right to be whoever she likes, and needs no defendants. I am not the defendant of the woman Fiorella. I am the accuser of a certain way to conduct rape trials. (Belmonti 1980: 59-61, my translation)

When compared to sexual violence, domestic violence has a different history regarding its relationship with the law. Despite the fact that struggles against domestic violence are clearly linked to those against sexual violence, the main focus regarding intimate partner violence has been the creation of women's shelters, rather than changing the law itself. The relevant article of the Criminal Code—formerly named *maltrattamenti in famiglia o verso fanciulli* (familial or child abuse)—has recently been modified in response to rising awareness of the issue of gender violence.[16] Yet

16. The law decree of 2013 makes it obligatory to inform the victim of violence if there is a request submitted to waive or

the nature and the structure of the crime, as well as the crucial features of the regime of mandatory prosecution—which does not hold in crimes of sexual violence—are left essentially unchanged. The article on domestic violence in the Rocco Code refers to a need felt at the time of its compilation: to protect victims who press charges in a context where the family and the social environment were likely to subject them to exceptional pressure to withdraw those charges. Clearly the 'best intentions' of the law were disengaged from the politics of social change regarding women's freedom, so as to produce a subject of rights non-autonomous by definition, a *minus habens* subject who is literally in need of the state in order to hold her stance. This stance regarding the law had thus to be taken once and for all, with all the resulting consequences: essentially, the female subject required by the Code is either a passive victim or a heroine who speaks out. In general, the rationale of the law on abuse expresses an interest in eliminating the ambivalence. This implies that in cases of partner violence the withdrawal of statements is much more common than in other crimes. Women's reluctance to make allegations and to press charges, and their possible reservations about going through with judicial processes, resulting in renouncements and retractions, are dealt with not through actions supporting those women but through institutional decision-making that does not provide for their reservations (Virgilio 2016). The juridical protection of abused women supposes that women are either free subjects or weak and passive agents; such a dichotomy is not found anywhere else

---

replace the restraining order against, or pre-trial detainment of, the aggressor before the final ruling. It also establishes that the preliminary investigation can never take longer than one year and that abuse victims have the right to legal counsel paid for by the state, regardless of their income, as well as tougher sentences and mandatory arrest for *in flagrante delicto* cases.

in the penal code. The rationale that underlies the category of crimes of mandatory prosecution conceives of the subject that suffered the violence in a very specific way. What mandates prosecution is not just the seriousness of the crime but also the definition of its victim, whose subjectivity in mandatorily prosecutable crimes is substituted for by the state, since her decisions cannot be taken as reliable.

During my court observations, intimate partner violence met a general tendency to normalize violence through the trivialization of domestic conflict, with the defense often using a simplifying and gender-blind language. For instance, the defense systematically replaced terms such as "violence" or even "conflict" with words such as "squabble," "scuffle" or "predicament," and frequently used impersonal expressions to describe episodes of violence—"some slapping occurred"—in an overall trend towards trivializing the violent event and denying its gendered dimension. While the statute of killing by honor was abolished in Italy in 1981, the theme of jealousy remains relevant in abuse trials. The defense seeks in particular to underline the 'human' and commonplace aspects of jealousy, rendering it explicitly as an ethical rather than legal concern. Judgments show a general tendency to undervalue violence, to deny its persistence, and to discredit women's words in the absence of evidence. The picture is further complicated by the extremely long procedure times of the Italian justice system,[17] and the established practice of granting mitigating circumstances, and consequently a suspended sentence, to defendants without prior criminal records. Honorary judges (honorary deputy attorneys) represent the prosecution in domestic violence hearings. They often change from hearing to hearing, ignore the details of the documents in the casefiles for the preliminary

17. Hearings are frequently postponed for diverse reasons, and often for months, on average 6-7 months. The testimonies that I observed concerned events that had occurred from two to four years earlier.

hearings, and are not experts on the subject. Women who do not have legal representation find themselves in court without being adequately prepared. The verification by the public prosecutor of the existence of different charges does not happen as a matter of course. Unless the victim's lawyer has them all gathered in one file, multiple charges against the same partner over time end up readily in the hands of different public prosecutors, and are treated separately in different proceedings.

The ambivalence involved in the intimacy of the relationship between the woman and the perpetrator often determines the dynamics of the legal procedure. In one case, the defense asked the plaintiff in court if the accused's threat to kill her with scissors and then turn them on himself, while falling to his knees in front of her, was "a theatrical gesture to demonstrate his feelings of love." Very tense, she answered in the affirmative. She smiled at her young lawyer only when the judge gave a suspended sentence as expressly requested by the prosecution.[18]

The trial can be experienced as an ordeal for the injured party as it constitutes the public exposure of an intimate relationship and its failure. In addition, the exhibition of the woman as a victim of violence, the potential meeting with her ex-partner, and possible judgments about her capacity as a mother and as a partner, all contribute to her potential distress. Through an ethnographic study conducted in Trinidad, Lazarus-Black identifies how courtroom rites can be seen as "secularly stylized events" (2007: 92) relating to domestic violence, expressing a power that reproduces itself, including apparatuses of intimidation, humiliation, objectification, silence, and judicial discretion. In the case of Carla, reported at the beginning of this chapter, the defense asked her to confirm that she had children by different partners, that she fled home when pregnant at seventeen, and about her contacts with social services and

18. Field notes, February 2, 2011.

her relationships with her parents and siblings, adding, "I don't want to give you a grilling, but you are the only witness against the accused."

Yet the problem with applying the charge of *maltrattamenti in famiglia* lies not only in a lack of recognition, in an undervaluation of violence, in the victim's hesitation to pursue justice, or in overly light sentencing. How a lack of recognition is produced is more complex than simple disregard or prejudice, or the little attention and sensitivity given to the context that produced the violence. In fact, the modalities of the judicial procedure raise a number of questions as to the possibility of eliciting the truth from the speaking subject. Modern law has been thought of as marked by a Weberian formal rationality, structured by general rules, in opposition to traditional and religious institutions (Silbey 2008: xi). Its logics have been criticized for being based upon devices that identify immediate causes, in order to produce facts and evidence, while dismissing enabling structures. Historically, legal thought and anthropology have followed distinctive paths. In particular, the attention to constitutive ambiguity and to the complexity of real-life situations that distinguishes anthropology is not to be found in the practice of making judgments. Legal thought depends on the adversarial nature of legal proceedings, which require yes/no answers, instead of the "yes but" of anthropology (Clifford 1988: 321). In general, anthropologists find legal approaches too unconcerned with the broader context, for they disregard "what are deemed extraneous details, in order to identify the abstract, general, *de*-contextualised legal principles assumed to lie concealed within" (Good 2007: 19). Analyses of the sociocultural aspects of law tend to separate and oppose the apparatus of power on the one hand and how power is understood and felt in everyday lives on the other; moreover, they usually underplay how law is implicated in the circulation of violence in social systems (Greenhouse 1995: 110).

Rather than "reducing narratives of conflict by the simple dichotomization of perpetrators and victims" (Eckert 2016), the legal management of domestic violence in Italy seems to rely on a peculiar inversion in which the proof of the crime is constituted by the intimate relationship, the experience of violence, and the consciousness of the abused victim. It is precisely the questioning of the simple dichotomization of perpetrator and victim that makes the victim's testimony untrue. Whereas "the force of 'law' cuts into a limitless expanse of 'justice,' reducing it and rendering it expressible, creating in the legal judgment a manipulable object of use" (Strathern 1996: 522), the verification of the crime of *maltrattamenti* makes the object of legal judgment impossible to manipulate because it revolves around a story told by the victim, the story of the abuse. Rather than passing through a process of selective omission and simplification, the crime is inserted within a story, meaning that the facts to be proven become even more unpredictable. It is not so much a question of having "to prune away" details (Good 2007: 19), but rather of reintroducing them into the legal analysis constantly. This occurs in the production of evidence by linking the facts—the facts of a violent event for which, almost by definition, there is no proof, for it happens in an intimate relation, in private space, and is diluted over time—to their cluttered context: the intimate story, wavering states of affection and conflict, continuous violent conduct. Intimate partner violence is a *sui generis* crime that needs to be identified by explaining more than necessary, instead of just ascertaining the violent events. This happens not despite but exactly because of how the testimonial evidence is based on a *superstes*, a survivor, who is called upon to describe the facts from first-hand experience and intimate narrative. It is precisely the acknowledgement of the context by the law, the awareness that this subject is not simply a figure in a trial but a gendered individual with a story, that prevents her from being recognized in legal terms. The shift to a moral discourse of responsibility opens the way to the private life of the subject through their interpellation: a person is not only a victim, a victim also has to be recognized as a person. The potential to know a victim-subject cannot but include the broader context that constitutes the subject as such: behind the victim there is a person, behind the person there is a victim, and neither of them acts as an analogy of the other. If the ways in which the law gains knowledge of a crime are depersonalizing, substituting one type of knowledge for another (Greenhouse 2017), what is implied by the introduction of *repersonalization* into such a framework, which does not provide for it? The foundational element of the law that allows for placing everything into a coherent framework is related to the possibility of dropping "almost everything" (Latour 2010: 264). So what happens when the personal story and the gendered relationship become the space for identifying crimes in legal terms? The attempt to contextualize violent events, in the in-depth analysis of the history of a relationship, leads to the potentially infinite investigation of the victim's experience and subjectivity. Not only does the evidence become that of the victim's life experience, caught up in a contingency that cannot be formalized, but the ambiguity of the feelings, the under- and over-determination of the victim, end up being an excess that must be taken up by the law but cannot be processed by it.

The Experience of Intimate Partner Violence: A Crime with a Story

According to lawyers from the shelter, as well as to the literature on the topic (Merry 1995), trials for domestic violence are considered to be banal, pointlessly complicated, and of little interest; in short, they are 'garbage' cases. Furthermore, they may result in a proliferation of charges and countercharges. In the context of the Italian justice system, which is structurally incapable of keeping to schedule, this widespread perception of irrelevance becomes decisive. The dynamics I observed in court highlight the domestic dimension, demonstrating the legal irrelevance both of much of what witnesses say and of defense questions. They also make clear the time-wasting involved in a context that is already overburdened with more significant crimes still awaiting trial. The following illustrates the atmosphere I observed often during hearings:

> Behind the desk: the judge; the registrar who is transcribing; and a young person looking bored who is in charge of a recording device and is chewing gum. The plaintiff is a man and the accused is a woman, who is absent. This is a countercharge after three charges for abuse and battery made by the accused against her ex-partner. The judge, a man around forty, sighing, says, half-laughing: "All right, it looks as if we were in a telenovela," interrupting the defense lawyer, who is going into too much detail about the arguments between the couple during the testimony of the mother of the ex-partner of the accused. The judge, looking bored and irritated, asks the witness to specify what she is referring to when she mentions the threats that the accused made to her son. She says that the offender often used to tell him, "you are disgusting." "Is that a threat?" asks the judge. The witness stresses the woman's mood swings. The judge says: "We all have those." The witness says her son was bitten, but the lawyer argues that the emergency room only documented redness to the neck and highlights that the woman is very slight and as such it is almost impossible that she could assault a man. The witness goes on: "I always told her how thin you've got, make sure you eat something." The second witness is a policeman (carabiniere) who says he read a message on the phone of the plaintiff (the ex-partner) that reads, "I love someone else, you don't mean anything to me."

> The judge sighs and, while listening, leans his head on his hand.[19]

The penal code in Italy forbids questions about the private life or the sexuality of the injured party if they are unnecessary to the reconstruction of the facts. However, domestic violence is not like other crimes; it is a crime that *needs* a story. In this respect, the following brief exchange I had with a young woman at the shelter is emblematic. From the opening question in the interview at the anti-violence center, in which she is asked what brought her there, her story dominates:

Gloria: The fact that, it happened that… a month before actually… No, I'm getting all mixed up in my head now [*long pause*]. I have to tell you the story of what happened between him and me.
Gribaldo: Tell me the story, yes please.
Gloria: At the beginning he made me feel like a queen [...][20]

The need to investigate the relationship with the law and the possibility of charges led to stories about the paradox of the law being interfering and yet impotent, of social services and the violence implied in their practices, and of a general context of judgments being made about the victim. The resistance to speak about violence lies in the contradiction inherent in intimate violence, the intimacy at issue being a chosen one, an intimacy that implies both choice and desire. These women have embodied a perception of intimacy with a liberal stress on self-responsibility and freedom. They are victims who see themselves as guilty for not knowing how to react to a context of power abuse considered to be obsolete in a society presumed egalitarian. They are therefore subject to pathologizing judgments about the apparently

19. Field notes, October 13, 2010.
20. Interview with Gloria, Casa delle donne, Bologna, June 2010.

outdated nature of their situation. The cultural possibility of expressing the experience of intimate violence in Italy relies also on the very chosen intimacy that modernity implies, involving self, responsibility, and emancipation (Plesset 2006). Stories of seduction and extremely subtle strategies of abuse, explosions of violence, blackmail, victimization, blaming, self-blame, the thin line between the real and the imagined, between right and wrong, between meaning and meaninglessness: not only do these experiences often evade effective narration, with a functioning chronological order and legal relevance, but the victims often have trouble themselves in fully understanding them, in that the complete and unambiguous meaning of these events corresponds to a mode of shared interpretation. In the words of a woman who after being heavily battered was told by her couples therapist to go back home to sleep, addressing herself to the women's shelter was an attempt to escape violence and at the same time to understand just what was happening to her: "I need to find out the boundary between the good and the evil, I was flirting with insanity because I did not know at that point who was crazy and who was not, and this damned fine line [...] I've been trying to preserve my perceptions."[21] Recurrent expressions such as "Do you understand what I am saying?" and "What effect does it have on you?" remark the victims' own perception of the difficulty in being believed.

Only after multiple precautionary strategies can the victim find a way out of a violent relationship. The narration is focused on their taking responsibility for their actions, actions which are often denied in the social perception of the victim of domestic violence. The stories I collected

21. Interview with Teresa, a woman who has been very in love with her husband and who decided not to press charges. In her account she recalls the "wonderful sensation" of being believed at the women's shelter. Casa delle donne, Bologna, June 2010.

hardly ever speak directly of violence. Rather, they speak of its conditions, of the way it spread out into the relationship, of their lack of autonomy, of the violence of the institutions. The relationship with the partner or ex-partner is central, as well as the victim's own ability to organize their life in a situation of emergency, and the ways in which they do that. The stories linger on the things that they have been able to do strategically to improve their economic and legal situation while they rediscover some meaning in life. They explain the grief at the end of the relationship. They highlight how they constantly mediate safe spaces and distance, in the complicated work of dealing with violence. As a consequence, they speak little of their experience of violence in the strict sense (where and when, the ways, the seriousness, the physical consequences). What is relevant to those who suffered violence does not necessarily correspond with what is relevant for the penal system.

The experience of domestic violence is not a precise event but rather a dynamic inserted into a continuum: when in court, victims are asked to demonstrate the repeated character of the action, because this is a criminal action with a past. The discrepancies between the demands of the court and the victim's testimony are not caused solely by the element of intimacy associated with the domestic sphere, which has historically been conceived of as private and not formalized in legal terms (Cavina 2011). Social services and legal professionals insist on a suitable and consequential representation of the facts, a requirement that brings into play a certain mastery of linguistic, cultural, and class-based tools (Mertz 1994), and in which the partner's violence is considered independently of the structural violence of a given social context (Adelman 2004). In order to demonstrate continued conduct, judges must be presented with accounts of repeated instances of violence, each one unique, specific, and detailed. It is difficult to meet this requirement because victims often employ a common type of narration in stories of domestic violence.

During hearings, I observed victims engage most frequently in one of two testimonial approaches. On the one hand, they offer *generic temporal narratives*—"he has always acted like that," "he has always treated me badly"—describing a behavioral mode instead of specific actions. On the other hand, they offer *kernel narratives*, lacking in detail, that briefly describe an action or a subject (Trinch and Berk-Seligson 2002), and do not lend themselves to constituting evidence. Indeed, "the law usually does not permit a witness to prove what happened on one occasion by reference to other, similar occasions" (Conley and O'Barr 1990: 17). The judge and the public prosecutor insist on the repetition of the violent acts in an effort to verify the duration and the frequency of abuse: "since when?" "how long?" "how often?" and "with what intensity?" are recurring questions. However, the woman's testimony often fails to satisfy the court's demand to precisely demonstrate the number, duration and frequency of acts of violence. Indeed, her testimony must often be reformulated by the judge. In the face of muddled accounts that do not correspond to a trial logic (Judge: "You must answer the question. If you do not remember, state that you do not remember"), what ends up being staged is a sort of fictionalization of the woman's precise memory of how often she was hit (Judge: "Well, let's say it was every two months"). The problem lies in the very fact that the woman's testimony does not attempt to meet the judge's requests. It does not lend itself to formalization and is continuously caught up with experiential and contingent elements.

In the following extract from a hearing, as in many other cases, the manner of the injured party is precisely what is considered most important. It occurred after more than two hours of incomplete and contradictory testimony, accompanied by outbursts of weeping from the victim. Here the questioning took a turn towards judging the woman herself, even though she was clearly uncomfortable and tired. The prosecutor's questions focused specifically on the key features of the romantic relationship in the context of physical and psychological violence: her feelings of affection despite the violence, the psychological weakness brought about by the abuse, her failure as a mother. Questions about the facts gave way to questions about the inconsistent and unreasonable behavior of the victim. The trial was about events from four years earlier. The woman pressing charges was in her mid-forties, and attempted suicide after suffering violence at the hands of her former partner. She looked tired and miserable, and sometimes seemed to literally be hanging onto a small bag she kept on her lap. Her words revealed traces of financial and health concerns, and more generally of a structural violence that could not be taken into account during the trial. This was one of the few hearings in which the defendant was present: he sat in the front row near the lawyer, wearing an everyday outfit of grey suit and white shirt and looking much younger than the plaintiff. He came off as calm and cheerful as he chatted with the witnesses for the defense sitting near me. Because of the way the seats were arranged, the victim sat very close to the defendant when testifying. The public prosecutor and the judge were women.

Public Prosecutor: Let's get back to the holiday in the year X. What happened?
Witness: I don't know what happened, I couldn't say anything. We were at his brother's house, with his mother. I was not able to talk to him for the entire vacation. I had to hold my tongue.
PP: What did he say to you?
W: Piece of shit, loser, worthless person…
PP: What triggered this behavior?
W: I don't know. I've asked myself the same thing many times.
PP: [*Impatient*] But, did he insult you? Do you mean he tended to ignore you?
W: He called me idiot, he went on and on for hours, it was psychological violence. My reaction was to remain silent.

PP: Would he become violent if you responded?
W: He would hit me.
PP: In what context? How many times, under what circumstances?
W: He put me down every day, it was psychological torture, he found it entertaining.
PP: And the blows? How often did they happen?
W: Two or three times a month, at least.
PP: In what circumstances?
W: If I resisted.
PP: But how did he hit you? You have to tell us, otherwise the judge will not believe you!
W: He slapped me, punched me, how can I describe it…
PP: Where?
W: On my belly, mainly… so not to leave bruises.
[…]
PP: Did these blows ever result in any injury?
W: He broke my arm, I had to tell people I had fallen down the stairs.
PP: When did that happen?
W: [*Bluntly*] I don't know. I have the report at home.
[…]
PP. Before or after [date]?
W: I don't remember.
PP: You have to tell us what happened and how he broke your arm.
W: He grabbed it, he broke it.
PP: But how? With his hands? With what?
W: With his hands.
[…]
Defense: Did you ever express the desire to commit suicide to X?
W: Yes.
D: On [date] you were heard by the police saying, "This is the first time that I have tried to commit suicide and I have never expressed my intentions to X."

W: No. I don't remember the police. The signature could be mine. I was taking psychiatric drugs and morphine. I can only say that it doesn't seem right…
Judge: [*Irritated*] You cannot say whether something is right or isn't right, say only that you don't remember. […]
J: Did his insults come out of the blue? For no reason?
W: He called me ignorant, fucking loser, idiot.
J: But when he started, wouldn't you ask him why?
W: He said he was just like that… he made scenes…
J: Listen, you have to be clearer. You must have asked him what the problem was.
W: I don't know how it started…[22]

Due to the importance of demonstrating that the conduct is continuous, a short circuit is created between rule-oriented accounts that address specific rules and principles and relational accounts dealing with social relationships and social status (Conley and O'Barr 1990). Whereas the prosecutor and judge focus more consistently on the how and the when of the violence, and the defense more consistently on the why, both sides nonetheless pose multiple questions to the injured party that are clearly aimed at verifying the reliability of her testimony: "what were the factors that caused the violence?" "suddenly?" "out of the blue?" The defense tends to use a less objective and contrived form of language, which is more similar to the testimony provided by violence victims themselves, and which delves more deeply into the intimate and experiential dimensions of the relationship. The judge and public prosecutor display a 'neutral' orientation aimed at identifying quantitative parameters for evaluating violence: parameters that, as we have seen, are not easily satisfied by women's narratives. Outside of this orientation, however, is a terrain that the defense often wields in an effort to draw attention to the nature of the couple's relationship. Not only

22. Field notes, November 18, 2010.

the violence but also the relationship itself is recreated in the courtroom, produced by the questions, elicited on the basis of reconstructed and resignified fragments. During the hearings, in an effort to prevent digressions and irrelevant statements, and so to proceed with a linear testimony, the public prosecutor invites the victim to "start from the beginning," which effectively coincides with the moment she met her partner. In treating the crime as having a story—a story about the intimate, domestic, familial life of the couple—it is the story that is interrogated. Supported by the judges and public prosecutors, the relationship-oriented dynamic of the woman's narration leads to an impasse.

The intimate space in which the violence took place constitutes the element that itself prevents the account from unfolding within the parameters required by the prosecution, and legal operators are then called on to manage lengthy narratives and unavoidable digressions. When the court does recognize the woman's need to position events within the framework of the relationship with the perpetrator, this nonetheless proves problematic in that this account is often rambling, disorganized, and not focused on the violent acts in question. The following is from a hearing that involves a plaintiff who withdrew a previous statement but then pressed further charges.

It is a morning when the court is, as it often happens, late with the daily schedule. The hearing, planned for 11 a.m., more than two hours later has not even started yet (other trials had to conclude first: a case of a car accident and one of illicit appropriation). At 1:30 p.m., the woman judge leaves for ten minutes, apparently for a quick lunch. I observe two people sitting a few seats away. They are the victim (the plaintiff), who is an Italian woman in a second marriage with a foreign man, and the male perpetrator (her husband, and the defendant) in the domestic violence hearing to follow. They sit next to each other. She loudly grumbles that she regrets forgiving him and that he is a liar, while he ignores her. She turns to the defendant's lawyer (a man), who stands silently in front of them. The judge returns, and the female public prosecutor calls the plaintiff to give her testimony, which she reads with emphasis on the oath as if to underline her truthfulness.

Public Prosecutor: Do you know the accused?
Witness: He's my husband on paper; we married after living together for a few months…
PP: What kind of relationship were you in…
W: [*Interrupting*] I came from a situation of familial abuse with two adult children…
Judge: Pardon me, what do you mean by abuse?
W: That I come from an abusive background.
J: Which, however, is not related to the facts that we're talking about…
W: [*In a complaining tone*] I was certainly not looking for that. I had a good relationship with him, and my daughter was our witness at the wedding.
PP: Explain more clearly…
W: In the year [given], I had a job, and we decided to live together. It was lovely, we were friends, we had many things in common, but after the wedding it gradually got worse … he worked cash in hand for a security firm who exploited him and so I provided for him…. He stayed out night and day without warning me. I was initially very worried and so he said to me, "You are mad," "You mustn't say anything to me," insults, a slap, a punch, and many times I didn't go to work because I had a black eye… love is not enough [*Turning towards the defense lawyer*].
J: You mustn't talk about other things!
W: I was speaking to the lawyer…
J: You have to answer the questions.[23]

23. Field notes, December 9, 2010. The trial is badly handled by a seemingly inadequate public prosecutor, who is frequently

When constraints are imposed on witnesses by the court—not to comment on their reactions or sentiments related to the reported events, not to digress, not to use comments about the possible state of mind of the people involved in the reported events, not to express value judgments, not to comment on the questions that are being put to them—the narration of the experience loses its meaning; it is no longer the narration of an experience. It is precisely the moment of going into detail about the life of a woman who is the victim of violence, the intricacies of her life, which poses a problem for the judge. Answer the questions, do not ramble, speak only when questioned, and stick to the facts: the court demands that testifying victims follow all of these guidelines.

Reconstructing the crime through a formalization and standardization of events is a central element of jurisprudence. However, in contexts that must account for intimate partner violence, courtroom dynamics reveal that this fundamental element can become very puzzling, as it is exactly the life story that makes the facts significant. If, as we have seen, violence is not directly talked about in the stories of the victims who ask for help in the women's shelter, the narration required during trial is on the contrary concentrated on the experience of violence as the central interest of the court. If this does not clearly emerge from the stories of the victims, the questions take another turn; what now come to fore are the relationships the woman has with herself, with her experience, and with her awareness of violence. The attestation of the violence suffered moves to the intertwining of the definition of a passive and de-responsibilized victim with respect to the charge (the conditions of the mandatory prosecution), the necessity that she talk about the violence (being interpellated to speak in court), and the verification that she interprets violence

---

interrupted by the judge in order to ask her own questions directly.

as such (her awareness). The relationship between the experience of violence, the speaking subject, and the proof of law, is caught up in a web of contradictory meanings.

In the next chapter I focus on the court investigation of the victim's experience and the meaning that she attributes to the violence and the motive that produced it. These elements are at the core of the demonstration of proof, creating a victim-subject that the law must recognize in order to be able to identify the crime that she has suffered.

CHAPTER THREE

Confessing Victimhood

Let's just say, without being too aggressive, that truth does not make law's life any easier, and especially not penal law.
Michel Foucault, 2014

The courtroom is a place of speaking where the voices of those who dare to venture are put to the test.
Antoine Garapon, 1997

Evidence and Testimonial Proof

Recent insights into the workings of legal systems have highlighted how the interpretation of narratives delivered in the trial phase plays a key role in determining the ruling: the construction of proof depends on an "ill-defined agglomeration of belief" made up of information, models, speculation, expectations, and prejudice (Twining 2006: 338). The investigation of doubt and proof has illustrated how judgments involve beliefs about types of truth and the weighing of evidence as a process of assessment through appeal to common experience (Berti, Good, and Tarabout 2015). Also relevant is the sequence of events between the production of evidence and the attribution of experience. In order to understand the multiple layers of testimonial evidence, I focus on the way legal judgment depends on witness statements about experience *as* evidence, by analyzing the relation between three elements required by institutions: what is being narrated, what the person who testifies experienced, and the violent events themselves.

The importance granted to a woman's testimony opens up a space in which the court issues multiple requests that help to define the female plaintiff's behavior through questions and assumptions that lead to the eliciting of a testimony where she must persuade the court. In other criminal proceedings, judicial evidence establishes motives or proves that a crime has been committed by a given perpetrator. Yet in this case the process of ascertaining facts shifts to the credibility of the victim herself. The construction of this figure in legal terms is so demanding and contradictory that it is actually impossible for the witness to meet the expectations involved. To ascertain the facts, it becomes crucial to understand the *meaning* of violence. Most important is the need to clarify the intentions and the motives of the perpetrator of violence, which must be explained by examining the victim. This extract from an interview with a female prosecutor clarifies the challenge from a juridical point of view:

> There is also the problem of making these factual situations correspond to the criminal circumstances in the light of all the jurisprudential interpretations that have been made, so the account must be given in detail and this makes it even more difficult. These crimes are particular for this reason as well… sometimes the victims of abuse cannot tell you how many times it happened, whether there were periods of interruption such that it was not habitual. The interruption does not exclude the possibility that it occurred. However, it is always necessary to verify why they took place, why they

> were interrupted, why they resumed, whether there was *animus proprio* [intentionality], an intention to oppress the other party, or if there were other motivations; and then you have to explain these sentences, so you have to ask a series of questions ...and there is the difficulty, the difficulty for us, but also for those who must then provide the material on which to base a decision, well, I don't think it will ever be resolved...I mean, we do get convictions and this kind of crime is dealt with, but I think it is more affected than others by the difficulty of reconciling the instruments in question...like ours, our categories with life...it is hard to frame it.[1]

In theory, the ritual form of the legal process should protect the accused (and the victim who speaks) more than the common practice of the social services. A peculiarity marks its structure and logics, its *externality*. The following reflections by Garapon hint at the sense of law's formalities: "The judicial ritual, its forms, its game, its exteriority, has something more respectable for the accused than the apostolic world of social work. Is it not better to ask an accused to simulate than to invade his 'secret garden'? Is it not an aggression to understand someone in spite of themselves?" (Garapon, quoted in Latour 2010: 265). Nonetheless, the rationale of the system that attempts to prove the crime is intrinsically violent towards women who have suffered violence: the closer the examination of her testimony, the less convincing it becomes. The prosecutor and the judge raise questions and comments meant to frame the testimony of witnesses, and that of the injured party in particular. Beginning from the victim's inability to report the crime, an attempt emerges to map out the crime by certifying the experience of the victim, so as to make it

1. Interview with female public prosecutor, Office of Procura, Bologna, April 2011.

a speech act in the broad sense. However, the experience continues to remain somehow unintelligible.

As discussed in Chapter Two, there are many reasons why women do not report, or hesitate to press charges against, a perpetrator. Among these, the lack of evidence plays an important role. The decision of culpability has to be reached on the basis of the judge's *intima convinzione*, a firm inner belief. A woman judge, encouraged to reflect on several cases when she had to face a weak and contradictory witness whose evidence could not be verified, insisted that a judge has the chance to understand better by questioning a witness during the final phase of a trial. Nonetheless, she finally admitted that it is impossible to overturn the outcome of a compromised trial, and eventually remarked:

> I might be convinced that my witness was telling the truth, but if she contradicted herself [...] or was not accurate about certain things, I might not have sufficient evidence to say that facts have been proven. Therefore, it cannot have a bearing on my decision. About being convinced, I mean the impression I have, let's say it is an inner conviction [*intima convinzione*].[2]

The definition of conviction beyond reasonable doubt is far from simple. The issue of the affective and experiential aspects to a judge's decision is not new to anthropology (Kobelinsky 2015). The idea of inner *personal* conviction calls into question the credibility of the judge's decision, as it seems to be at odds with the usual firmness required in legal judgments, being more linked to moral sense and intuition than to rational thinking. Deep-seated conviction means conviction in a purely subjective sphere, that of the inner self. The potential credibility of the witness, which

2. Interview with female judge, Office of Criminal Court, Bologna, March 2011.

produces the effective, personal conviction, is lost in the course of narration. During the testimony, the evidence loses the sufficient elements required to be upheld. Trust cannot lead to conviction, which has different truth criteria.

The aspect evoking clarity of vision in the word *evidence*, which derives from the Latin verb *videre* (to see), does not exclude ambiguities in a Romance language such as Italian. Indeed, in Italian the word *evidence* is translated differently depending on the context. In legal terms, it is usually translated as *prova* (proof). While the term *prova* is linked to demonstration, the term *evidenza* (normally used in the adjectival form, *evidente,* meaning "clear") has a rather different meaning. It is something that does not provide instances of proof, in that it indicates what is already clear, apparent, evident, and persuasive. In the Italian legal system, the notions of *prova* and *evidenza* are therefore closely related but do not overlap. *Prova* can be quite evident, as in the case of an arrest *in flagrante delicto*—here again, the Latin root has connotations of blazing, brightness of seeing—but it may also be non-evident, that is, requiring further support. In other words, evidence is a qualification of proof that is relevant only insofar as the law seeks to achieve certain outcomes, usually a sentence, on the basis of this proof, without the need for additional procedures. Despite its importance, the law does not establish any specific requirements for *evidenza.* It might be considered such even if it is subject to only one means of testing; or, vice versa, a case may present multiple proofs that are in agreement with one another and yet not considered by the judge to constitute evidence, as they are not sufficiently unambiguous and therefore not persuasive enough. This duality can also be found in the vocabulary of the common law. One of the most widely read North American procedural law treatises on evidence refers to the burden of proof as composed of two distinct parts. The first consists of the burden of producing evidence regarding a specific fact that is in dispute, while the second involves persuading the judge that the fact in question is true, that is, the burden of persuasion. This point highlights the relationship between proof and evidence:

> *Proof* is an ambiguous word. We sometimes use it to mean evidence, such as testimony or documents. Sometimes, when we say a thing is 'proven' we mean that we are convinced by the data submitted that the alleged fact is true. Thus, 'proof' is the end-result of conviction or persuasion produced by the evidence. (McCormick 1954: 635-636)

Among the forms of proof required by law, such as real evidence and documentary evidence, the testimonial proof of a woman who has suffered intimate partner violence represents a particular case. In testimonial proof of domestic violence, the burden of producing evidence and the burden of persuading are not only mutually implicated but may exist in a relation of intractable contradiction. The plaintiff's testimonial evidence depends on the credibility of the narrative in which the victim's capacity to know and understand her own experience, and to act consequently, are simultaneously under investigation. In this context, testifying to a fact involves not only bearing witness to something she has observed, but also bearing witness to something she has experienced. This brings into play two dimensions. The first is the dimension of experience, in which a woman has to demonstrate that she knows what has happened, or is able to *read* her experience in a way that is consistent and aimed at righting a wrong (I declare myself to be a victim of violence, and I appear here as such and therefore demand justice in relation to the perpetrator). The second is the dimension of persuasion, in that she has to prove what she says is true, through an exhibition of this valid, conscious self/victim (what I say reflects my experience and, therefore, constitutes evidence).

The Burden of Evidence: Experience

Hearings abound with claims of "I don't remember;" silences, tears and embarrassment; accelerated narratives, broken by emotion; contradictions and oversights; and a tendency to ramble, to dwell on aspects that are irrelevant from a legal point of view. Efforts by the judge and public prosecutor to organize a plausible and consequential narrative from a woman's account create in the witness suffering, difficulty, further confusion, and a sense of powerlessness. The court perceives the witness's difficulty in remembering as an inexplicable scandal. This reaction comes not only from the defense, as we might expect, but also from the judge, as illustrated in the following:

Woman: I can't remember anymore, sorry, it was so long ago.
Judge: [*Irritated*] So, either you are trying to forget, or what happened didn't have an impact on your life. I am amazed that you are unable to remember these events. Considering that you were the one to press charges, you ought to remember. We are trying to judge the accused. A criminal trial has certain requirements. Even though you as a couple are no longer in conflict.[3]

The exchanges with the witness are inquisitive and aggressive, and the suggestion is that she is faking her responses and exaggerating her reactions, or putting them on for the occasion. Her hesitations and outbreaks of tears while remembering the episodes of violence are held up as demonstrations of her unreliability as a witness. Her

3. Field notes, December 13, 2010. This trial started from a charge not pressed directly by the victim but by social services. She has two children with the defendant and has been living with them in a shelter. The hearing is largely focused on verifying whether she is a good mother, including testimony of social services psychologists, as requested by the defense.

unreadiness to speak is understood as a desire to cover things up, or as her failure to take responsibility for what is being testified. In the context of trauma, processes of remembering and translating memories into words are highly problematic. They are subject to acts of suppression (Herman 1997), in which the narrative is blocked by the workings of the unconscious, where the victim feels not only that she will not be believed but also that she has been distanced from her own lived experience. The stories of the women I interviewed retrace the distance from traumatic experience, a physical pain that has had no time to be felt, to its recollection in court, where there is also no space for their perception of that pain in a communicable sense. A pain that does not have time to be expressed is a pain that cannot be legitimately experienced. Communication and experience collapse into each other:

> Because I, at that time, I tell you, I felt like I was in a coma. Can you believe it, I didn't feel physical pain. I was beaten almost every day, I didn't even have time to recover, or even to feel pain, not even, I didn't have time for anything, it was... That's how I remember myself, like a person that, and sometimes it seemed possible, if I look back to that time, it's like I'm looking at a dead woman. A woman that I know.[4]

There is a significant body of literature about memory and post-traumatic testimony that focuses on whether or not testimony is possible, and recognizes that trauma produces a crisis of representation (Caruth 1995; Felman 2002). The encounter between law and trauma makes language collapse, constructing a sort of judicial denial that "reflects and duplicates the constitutional blindness of culture and of consciousness toward the trauma" (Felman 2002: 5). Where

4. Interview with Linda, Casa delle donne, Bologna, September 2010.

embodied experience is entwined with structural violence and public discourse, battered women face the difficulties of remembering and giving a consistent shape to narratives of violence (Kirmayer 2007). Here, I focus on an element that appears to be as yet undertheorized: even before causing problems as a narrative, a woman's testimony raises problems at the level of the victim's experience. The questions she must answer include: Did you experience violence? In what way was it ongoing? What were the violent events, and what kind of violence was involved? These questions go unanswered, or the answers offered fail to meet the demands of the court. The failure to answer raises additional questions during the trial proceedings. Queries are posed as rhetorical questions that the court asks itself instead of the victim: Why does she not speak? Has she understood what the judge is asking her? If it was really that traumatic, why is she unable to remember? Silence in court requires an interpretation. The fragmented narratives not only speak to the women's inability to remember and recount, but they also call into question the very experiences of these women as events they really lived through. Judges' efforts to understand what these female witnesses mean contain the unanswered question: What has she experienced?

In my interviews with victims, experiences of violence and trauma do not overlap, and only a few stories that I gathered can be defined through the clinical language of trauma. Nonetheless, this particular relationship with experience and narration can be understood through insights into how trauma is experienced and expressed (Hastrup 2003; Good 2007). When testimony on experiences of violence enters into the institutional domain, and is therefore subjected to evaluation by experts in the medical and legal fields, the question of expressing violence according to the appropriate criteria becomes problematic. Fassin and d'Halluin (2007) have shown how, in the case of refugees, adapting to post-traumatic stress disorder as a diagnostic category ends up preventing the trauma itself from being recognized. Common sense supposes that traumatic events will be remembered vividly and precisely, just because they are decisive events. Thus, inconsistencies are viewed as proof of deception and lack of credibility, or of second-hand testimonies, against all medical (and anthropological) evidence demonstrating that detachment is a distinctive feature of traumatic memories. In particular, the feminist critique of the notion of trauma has stressed how, paradoxically, it is the very everydayness and repetitiveness of women's daily experiences of violence that make these experiences difficult to classify as trauma (Brown 1995). In his reports of cases of rape of detainees from Sri Lanka seeking asylum, Good (2007: 93) highlights how sexual violence in detention can be discarded, not so much because it is not deemed sufficiently serious, but rather because it cannot be inscribed straightforwardly under the category of torture or persecution, comprising as it does individual acts that are not condoned by local authorities.

The issue is not only the narrative or the ability to speak, but also the very nature of experience as a part of trial proceedings. Accounts of acts of violence are not only required to report the experience in the right way, through a suitable narrative. They also have to demonstrate that the victims have *properly experienced* the violence in question. Reporting one's own experience means giving evidence of the capacity to understand it correctly, and thus to act appropriately. If a woman is the only witness to an act of violence, it is not simply because she is the only person capable of recounting it, in the absence of other evidence or witnesses. She is also the only witness because it is her own subjectivity that determines the definition, perception, and experience of the act—whether physical or psychological—*as* an act of violence.

I detail an exchange that took place in the particularly animated hearing discussed at the end of Chapter Two.[5] The complaining witness was asked by the judge to leave the courtroom because she interrupted the defense, shouted,

5. See pp. 63-64.

cried, and responded to defense questions with her own questions. The public prosecutor tries to interrupt her ("You ended up in hospital several times. Why did you carry on living with him?"), the judge asks her to get back to the point ("Stop talking about other things!"), but she speaks over him, pointing out that the defendant is the accused, not her, and that she was also the victim of violence in her previous relationship. The defense latches onto this:

Defence: In order to give a picture of your previous relationship, I ask you if your partner abused you in your previous relationship.
Witness: I say it's not pertinent.
Judge: I am the one who decides if it's pertinent.
D: How come? Let me finish my question… how did you manage to live with your ex-partner?
W: I asked him to go away, but I don't have to answer you on questions about my ex…
J: No. He is asking you how come you stayed with him? Were there practical reasons?
W: Personal reasons that I don't have to list here. I remind you that my eldest daughter was a witness at my wedding…
J: But you don't have to remind him of anything!
W: I'm only asking for pertinence and respect.
D: On the [date] there was an indictment for abuse; she denounced her ex-husband numerous times…
W: [*Interrupts again*] I am wondering what is the pertinence of this!
J: We will suspend the hearing. It isn't possible to cross-examine in this way.
W: Me? Indictment? [*Agitated*]
J: When you have calmed down we will call you back.
W: [*Leaving*] Sort out your facts!
[...]
After a police officer delivers testimony on the messages that the plaintiff and the defendant exchanged, the judge lets the woman back in.

J: We will try to let the witness back in [*Turning to the defense*] please try not to go too far…
The witness enters
W: Sorry judge, I didn't sleep at all; I still feel things despite everything…
J: Never mind
[...]
W: [...] When he came back, I was scrubbing the floor. He broke the bowl, tipped the water over me and then he pushed me into the room and so on. He pushed me and beat me up.
D: What does "pushed" and "beat up" mean?
W: Look, there were so many that I can't remember all of them, I have never lied…
D: You say, "He punched me." Where?
T: Everywhere.
D: You said, "He punched me and threatened me," and what did you do at that point? How did you defend yourself? [*Here the lawyer becomes aggressive, almost shouting. The judge, trying to speak, attempts to stop him, meanwhile the witness interjects again.*]
W: I tried to get away from him!
D: [*In an ironic and contemptuous tone*] You got away from him and picked up the bowl? Why did you pick up the bowl? I don't understand!
W: You need to understand other things, sir. I am here because I forgave...
D: [*Cutting her off*] He threatened you…
W: [*Interrupting*] Yes, of course, and also….
J: Wait for the question before answering!
D: [*Shouting*] For these reasons you got a trauma to your ankle and noise-induced hearing loss…
W: Obviously you have never been beaten up. I have been and what I'm saying is true.

This exchange exemplifies different dynamics at play during hearings: the difficulty of keeping the narration within the requirements of the court; the insistence on past facts that regard the private life of the witness; the inexplicability of her failure to part from him. It is worth looking at the legal device for eliciting the violence by corroborating the victim's words, trying to better understand what is hidden in the defense question, "What does 'pushed' and 'beat up' mean?" This is not simply about a need to hear the details so as to show that the woman lied, that she is untrustworthy, that these are not violent acts. Behind this question lies another element: examining if the woman's experience of violence fits with the crime. The defense insists on the fact that she had already claimed having been the victim of violence by her ex-partner. The complaining witness refers to the fact that the defense lawyer has not had this kind of experience. Her own interpretation of violence is at stake. As shown in Chapter One, the contested issue in domestic violence (even in a quantitative framework) is the victim's perception, the objectification rendered through the social use of the term "violence," and the relationship between performer and witness. On the one hand, moving the focus from the actions of the perpetrator to the perceptions of the victim gives voice to the subject who suffered the violence. On the other hand, it risks putting the victim on trial, since it is precisely her perception that must be rendered as objective, and is therefore scrutinized. This illustrates a way of thinking that relates to "questions about certainty or doubt over our own pain or that of others" (Das 2007: 57). The legal context represents a challenge to the necessity of working out how to think about the body, about experience and pain, within the space of its certification in a court. Experiences of violence in intimate relationships involve certain constants that repeatedly emerged in my interviews with women who had suffered abuse, and in the accounts they offered at hearings. Not only do these experiences often evade effective narration, with functional chronological sequence and clear legal relevance. They are also something the victims themselves have trouble fully understanding, because the complete and unambiguous meaning of such events does not correspond to a shared interpretative mode. They generate responses that emphasize the overall difficulty that women face in framing their own experiences: in the courtroom, it is the experience itself that does not appear sufficiently evident and straightforward.

The issue of testimonial narrative is linked to the production of evidence through notions of knowledge and truth that focus on the victim's subjectivity. In this intersection, not only is her testimony investigated as evidence but also her ability to perceive her own experiences. In this respect, her capacity to know also comes under scrutiny. In their interactions with the legal system, the battered women I met suffer from what Fricker (2007) has termed epistemic injustice: a wrong committed against someone specifically in their capacity as a knower and giver of knowledge. Epistemic injustice takes two forms: hermeneutical and testimonial injustice. The former indicates a gap in collective interpretative resources that disadvantages a person when she is called upon to make sense of a social experience. The latter involves the low level of credibility attributed by the hearer to the evidence that the speaker is offering the truth (Fricker 2007: 12). Indeed,

> the social experiences of members of hermeneutically marginalized groups are left inadequately conceptualized and so ill-understood, perhaps even by the subjects themselves; and/or attempts at communication made by such groups, where they do have an adequate grip on the content of what they aim to convey, are not heard as rational owing to their expressive style being inadequately understood. (Fricker 2007: 6-7)

In the domestic violence trials I observed, this frame defines the ability to report a crime, an experienced wrong, in a way that is sequential and comprehensible, and even more so in a way that is shared and evident.

An example of this gap in interpretation and credibility can be seen in the definition of violence, starting from the experience of the victim, and especially in the relationship between physical and psychological violence. The law on domestic violence includes psychological violence even though there is no specific provision for it in the Italian judicial system. It can be punished in several guises: as private violence, threats, insults, or harassment. The dynamics in the courtroom generate a vision of verbal violence as part of 'normal' gender dynamics, a kind of interaction in which the partners are 'on the same level' and the woman is able to respond in kind. Physical violence, on the other hand, is framed as infantilizing. Physical violence is the aspect that clearly determines women's oppression at the hands of men, unquestionably marked by inequalities of status and power. Women who have experienced domestic violence do not always share this interpretation, however. As described in Chapter Two, the women I interviewed often skipped over the details of physical violence. The narratives I collected, both in the shelter and from courtroom observation, dwelt not so much on the beatings but rather, or particularly, on the state of mind resulting from violent acts. In testimony about episodes of violence, and how these were perceived by women victims, it is clear that what they define as violent is less the actual exercise of physical force as such, and more the psychological and verbal violence, repeated acts, continual aggression, and threats. What they foreground is the potential for physical violence, its justification, and its underlying ethos: "I am not afraid of battering because I already went through that and survived;"[6] "Bruises disappear, but it is psychological violence that is awful."[7] What repeatedly emerged in interviews, and even in courtroom

6. Interview with Giulia, Casa delle donne, Bologna, June 2010.
7. Interview with Cristina, a young woman with child, who pressed charges against the ex-partner and withdrew them several times, Casa delle donne, Bologna, July 2010.

testimonies, is the fact that, while the court focuses on physical violence, the women themselves do not necessarily think it the most important aspect of their experience.

A victim must demonstrate she is aware of the experience of violence she has endured, through insight, introspection, and ultimately the self-governance to develop a suitable knowledge of her feelings and the consequences of her choices and acts. Professionals seek to elicit this experience by beginning from a notion of awareness, an idea that combines the capacity for experience, judgment, and action. This entails an unproblematic view of emancipation as a "teleological story in which desire ultimately overcomes social control and becomes visible" (Scott 1991: 778). The authentic and self-evident subject therefore meets the legal need to give evidence of the experience of suffering. If rape trials deal with bodily submission—inasmuch as consent is debated in terms of physical desire, turning such an event into a "pornographic vignette" (Smart 1989: 39)—domestic violence trials revolve around victims' feelings and awareness: their stances towards and interpretations of intimate violence. As in rape trials (Matoesian 1993), victims of domestic violence are called on to communicate in the courtroom not so much the evidence of the facts as that they are indeed telling the truth; that is, the very fact of their credibility. In cases of domestic violence, though, this credibility is entangled with intimate feelings, with the way the victims themselves view and interpret intimate partner violence. The way they live the experience of violence is what makes them into truthful, authentic victims.

When Evidence Lies in the Victim Subject

The figure of the woman-victim, she who testifies to violence and who holds a central place in familial abuse trials, is constructed through intersecting lines of questioning and through assumptions that are articulated around the examination of the victim as an individual person (Schneider 1994). The courtroom dynamics are such that a woman who seeks recognition as a legitimate participant in the trial must constitute herself as a victim-subject and grant credibility to her testimony through the accounts she gives of herself. A typical example of the difficulty of overcoming these binary logics can be seen in the efforts of legal operators to problematize the fact that the female victim chose to stay with her violent partner. The more or less explicit iteration of the old question "Why didn't you leave him?" (Mahoney 1994: 76) fails to recognize that escaping an abusive relationship is a process and not a singular event (Chiu 2001: 1271):

[*The judge intervenes*] Judge: Were you in love?
Witness: Yes, yes, I loved him very much, I saw him as an intelligent person.
J: Even though he hit you?
W: Yes.
J: Why didn't you leave him?
W: He had taken everything away from me. I couldn't afford it.
J: Have you ever seen a psychiatrist for help?
W. No.
J: You said your daughter would shut herself in her room when you fought. Didn't you ever think you should have removed your daughter from this environment?
W: I was not up to it psychologically.[8]

The stay-or-leave dichotomy entails a judgment on the victim who has failed to escape her own (apparently perverse) relationship with the perpetrator. Expectations about the behavior of battered women create an equation linking their agency to the act of separation from the violent partner. Furthermore, this equation also implicitly

8. Field notes, November 18, 2010.

invokes the dichotomy between agency and oppression or victimization. Liberal understandings of freedom construe it as the capacity to enact authentic, autonomous will. Yet as Mahmood (2005: 8) points out, agency does not inevitably entail a subjectivity produced through opposition and "against the weight of custom, tradition, transcendental will, or other obstacles." In cases of intimate partner violence, a woman's innocence lies in not making claims, not loving, not hating, not acting; that is to say, being a victim and nothing more (Christie 1986). The power granted to a woman's words is disciplined through discourses that emphasize a victim's reliability, coherence, and, finally, innocence. The Italian legal field is a heterogeneous system of knowledge and power that engages in complex relations with techniques of subjection and discourses of truth. As such, it is eminently suited to investigating the production of the victim-subject.

Foucault (1975; 2014) has underlined the historical shift in criminal justice from judging the facts to judging the motive. The modern era thus focuses on investigating what triggered the crime, rather than on the urge to punish that follows from it. These novel hermeneutics of the subject create a new technique of interpretation too, such that the crime is no longer simply an act for which somebody can be charged but also becomes an act that is meaningful. The demand that the guilty subject confess is justified by the need to reveal not just the person who might be held to legal account for a crime, but also the subjectivity that has a meaningful link to that crime. The guilty party must be made to speak, such that this subjectivity can be taken up in discourses that are capable of codifying the motive and inscribing the crime into patterns in the subject's overall behavior.

In cases of domestic violence, however, a shift occurs in which the subjectivity of the injured party, rather than of the accused, takes center stage in the trial. The question "Who did what to whom and with what intentions?" often slides rapidly into a question that the woman is asked to answer: "Who are you?" During the hearings of familial abuse cases I observed, the device of confession was applied paradoxically to the victim instead of the perpetrator. Since the perpetrator of violence usually fails to appear in court, and therefore never takes the stand, his character quite literally comes to be played by the woman. He emerges only through statements made by others, and is never the object of what might be called identification processes. The testifying victim is called on to make a confession about herself in relation to her husband (an institutional figure), her lover (a relational figure), or her aggressor (a figure that must be assembled/discovered/judged). During hearings on domestic violence, women are pressured to tell the truth about themselves, a truth that takes shape through their relationship with the perpetrator of violence. In the end, the victim is asked to *speak for* the perpetrator, to clarify the reasons behind the crime. The perpetrator's actions only have sense in relation to the process of identifying the victim herself. He is judged guilty on the basis of her statements, and therefore she is the one who must grant meaning to his actions: "What led to his behavior?"

Even if violence is no longer thought legitimate within the family in Italy, assessing it in law nonetheless requires that it be made explicit and comprehensible. The role of the judge is to ensure that, while violence is never reasonable, it has to be explained for it to be verified. And this explanation must be given by she who suffered it. She is the one who best embodies the effort to interpret an otherwise meaningless act of violence, since the perpetrator does not attest any claim about its meaning. When it comes to violence, and especially structural violence such as gender violence, the interpretive labor is demanded of the powerless, not the powerful. The work of interpreting violence must be done, not by its perpetrators, but rather by those who suffer it: subaltern subjects identified as needing to understand the sense and the meaning of the violence exercised on them. Those who exercise it are not expected to make this effort

(Graeber 2012). In Chapter One I showed how victims' interpretations of violence cannot be taken into account in statistics because of the risk of jeopardizing objectivity. The paradox here is that the silencing of the victim's interpretation is then overturned in the space of the law. This establishes a subject who, in the moment she names the violence she has suffered, is interpellated to interpret it. The victim must supply a meaningful framework that allows for recognition and certification, making the production of evidence possible.

This demand to tell the truth about oneself, either following violence endured or in view of its future potential, has been widely explored in the anthropology of refugees (e.g., Beneduce 2015; Malkki 1996; McKinley 1997). Such confessional accounts demand that a person's life be re-formed to fit, recognizably, with a socially intelligible and politically available identity that proves the subject's degree of victimhood. Fassin (2013) has especially noted the paradox in the requirement that refugees demonstrate evidence of persecution in their home countries: increasing rates of refusal to grant refugee status serve as a defense of this same figure. The more judges are suspicious of claimants' evidence of potential or actual persecution, the more the principle of asylum acquires value (Fassin 2013). This shift in focus from the veracity of the account to the sincerity of the person, found in the trials of refugees, is also characteristic of the treatment of women's voices in trials for gender violence. The problem refugees encounter in testifying is also found in the bias against women's testimonies in domestic violence cases. In the case of refugees, the state recognizes past violence linked to another political-territorial context. In the case of domestic violence, it demands proof of violence suffered at the hands of an intimate partner within the territory of everyday domestic life. In both of these cases, however, the apparatus of confession is twisted. In order to become subjects with the right to recognition, safety, and compensation, *victims* must confess in an incontrovertible and verifiable way to having been objects of past violence. The difficulty of creating a link between violence against women and human rights is due to the necessity of defending the status of human rights as a canon in which the state is called to intervene (Charlesworth 1999). The courts feel the need to subject the victim to such scrutiny because the very ideal of the victim invokes the imaginary of the authentic target of violence deserving defense. Refugees are rendered less credible when they lack effective knowledge concerning persecutors' intentions (Bohmer and Shuman 2018: 23). In the case of domestic violence, that same lack of knowledge creates even more problematic effects because of the intimacy linking victim and perpetrator.

The act of speaking out—of reporting an incident and expressing one's experience as the victim of violence—is generally commended as a progressive political reference. Yet breaking the silence is not the only way that stories of violence can and must be made public. The idea that speaking clearly and pressing charges are the only means of expression creates its own harm. As Veena Das emphasizes, the boundaries between saying and showing when violence is expressed are to be protected from the imaginary of unveiling and unraveling:

> It is often considered the task of historiography to break the silences that announce the zones of taboo. There is even something heroic in the image of empowering women to speak and to give voice to the voiceless. [...W]hen we use such imagery as breaking the silence, we may end by using our capacity to 'unearth' hidden facts as a weapon. (Das 2007: 57)

Bearing witness to suffering, being seen to be listening, are frequently identified as privileged acts in a framework shaped by an ethos of compassion. The use of this framework has seen a sudden upsurge in recent years (Fassin and Rechtman 2007). Subjects learn to express their own inner being in words and images through techniques of governmentality that weave together state policies and psycho-pedagogical discourses (Rose 1989). These mechanisms also entail exposure to popular modes of expression, including those in the entertainment industry, that revolve around what is essentially an accumulation of discourse about the self, its discomfort and suffering, and the exploration of intimacy in relationships. The courtroom context for testimony by victims of intimate partner violence is likewise clearly affected by these forms of discourse that bring into play gender differences, the display of the self, proof of authenticity, and appeals for compassion. The relationship with speech is crucial: when intimacy becomes an issue, tacit fantasies, rules, and obligations are revealed, requiring a therapeutic eloquence (Berlant 1998: 287).

The institutions demanding that victims take personal charge for being aware of their situations and giving an account of them in court—institutions including psychiatry, medicine, and law—are implicated in the construction of domestic violence. The victim is the person who possesses the key to herself. Awareness of the violence suffered is the condition of her freedom, and therefore of her capacity to become an agent, discover the truth, and demonstrate it. Self-governance and reflexivity make testimony intelligible and legally significant. At the same time, however, the agency implied makes women suspect. Women who have the chance to speak, thanks to their steadfastness in pursuing their intent, but who fail to conform to the codes for expressing their suffering, run the risk of being judged for their ability to manipulate. If a woman wants the violence she has suffered to be recognized, she must constitute herself as a victim, conferring reality on the crime through a discourse that holds her together as a coherent subject. In her avowal the subject must play the role of being subjugated, adhering to what she is. Foucault's reflections on avowal are illuminating in this regard: "[The] avowal is not simply an observation about oneself. It is a sort of engagement, but an engagement of a particular type. It does not obligate one to do such and such a thing. It implies that he who speaks promises to be what he affirms himself to be, precisely because he is just that" (Foucault 2014, 16). So the person who is at the origin of the legal case speaks for the perpetrator, having had a significant intimate relationship with him, and given that he is legally subtracted from the requirement to speak. The perpetrator can speak only through the defense, producing an interiority as the accused which has less weight, removed as it is from the law—a perpetrator's jealousy, for example, being an ethical rather than legal question. The decisive and legitimate interiority is that of the plaintiff as subject of the law: the abused victim has the right to speak. The shift towards eliciting the violent act through the victim frees the perpetrator from the liability of being culpable. It liberates him from the condition that he must answer to the interpellation of the law, which defines whoever responds to it and is based on the assumption of psychological continuity and intentionality, or, in short, on moral interiority. In countries based on Roman law, truth and justice reference each other more substantially than in common law traditions: Garapon (1997) identifies the difference between the two systems in the attitude towards the testimony/avowal. In France, namely, the law is experienced as the prolonging of the benevolent action of the sovereign, or the superiority of the community with respect to individuals, the latter being such insofar as they belong to a political community. In common law, however, there is mistrust in relation to the avowal, along with protection from intrusion into the interior sphere, thus affirming the centrality of the rules of the social contract, individuals being masters of themselves. In the Protestant culture of common law, the idea of confession disappears together with those of release and redemption. In civil law systems, by contrast, the judgment of the magistrate must not separate the facts from the individual who is accused. The result is that judgment forms around the person instead of the facts, leading to the individualization of the punishment as against the common-law principle of equality.

In dealing with these themes of witness confession and the intimate beliefs of the judge, it is useful to look to recent anthropological concerns with trust and mistrust (Carey 2017), and with the very possibility of knowledge of others' minds, as a trait bound to cultural context (Robbins and Rumsey 2008). Confession is a critical site for exploring ideas concerning intentionality and the opacity of other subjects, since Western assumptions regarding intentions are crucial to the associated meanings of transparency and sincerity in speech. Though such studies do not engage with Foucault's analysis of confession and its developments, they emphasize how a possible disinterest in intentions and motivations stems from a distancing from the form of the confession found in the Christian tradition. Ethnographic work, especially in the Pacific, has shown how speech might be understood as unable to convey what lies in the minds of others or counteract their constitutive opacity (Robbins 2008). Describing unofficial courts in Melanesia, Strathern (1972; 2008) has also detailed the treatment of women's complaints. This focused on investigating the motivations for airing grievance and matters of disposition, rather than the issues that women's voices raised. In this respect, evidence for one's grievance was indeed taken as being evidence for a state of mind: evidence for one thing stood for evidence of another (Strathern 2008: 23).

During hearings I observed, an insistence on the reasons behind violent conduct led to a chain of investigations into such motives, in order to elicit evidence. Hearings focused on the experience of violence, on the reasons for the violence, and at the same time on the possible reasons for a woman's speaking out against a perpetrator. Her testimony, which is necessary to identify the crime, must *in primis* identify the victim. The process of interpellating her speech in court revolves on facts, experiences, intentions, and motivations. The abused woman is an opaque and ineffable figure. Although it is clear what she wants in her daily life outside of the institution, her relation with the law remains obscure. And if it seems difficult to understand what abused women want from the law, it is as difficult to understand what the law itself wants from them. In legal hearings for domestic violence cases, women are asked to talk about facts that are supposed to affect their own true, intimate selves. This is in order not only to verify the facts but to verify women's capacities to understand and communicate the intimate violence experienced. Testimony emerges as a specific device that investigates intentionality. The law is not content with reaching the meaning of human action. It also reflects a presumption to say something of experience. It shares this with an anthropology that analyzes public discourses, institutions, and products of human action (Robbins and Rumsey 2008: 417).

The practice of confession—"Tell the story,""Tell us why," "Take a position, and press charges"—participates in the device of proving the facts. This represents an odd betrayal of the requirement of judicial ritual, because it is not the accused but the complaining victim who speaks within the framework of a crime that itself constitutes her as a subject lacking authoritative voice. Telling the truth concerns, significantly, the truth about oneself, and the possibility of communicating an individual or collective subjectivity. The loose relationship with truth that is inherent to statements of personal history and inner intention can take on different meanings. This has been shown in contexts as diverse as the High Atlas in Morocco (Carey 2017) or among Hungarian Roma in France (Foisneau 2016). As a strategy for avoiding anti-Roma stigma in France, or as a way of conceiving inner worlds and personhood in Morocco, the act of declining to tell the true self in response to a demand to do so, whether that demand is relational, institutional, or social, opens space for a reflection on the meaning of subtraction as a principle that allows the recognition of a freedom, an autonomy, that obviously has gendered dimensions as well. A peculiar relationship exists between (un)trustworthiness and gender in the context Carey illustrates. The attribution to women in the High Atlas of a greater reliability when it comes to personal information relates to the fact that identifying an individual as potentially untrustworthy corresponds with the acknowledgement of autonomy (2017: 27-28, 35). In the context I describe here, the ambivalence of Italian law on domestic violence problematically makes autonomy and untrustworthiness coalesce. The relationship between trustworthiness and untrustworthiness is so ambiguous that the request of the law for the intimate truth of women who have experienced partner violence is a request that cannot be satisfied without lying, or rather, lying without intention to deceive (Carey 2017: 27). A form of subtraction before the request to express one's self can also be read as the possibility of not being found where norms expect to find you.

In the next chapter, I will suggest that self-reflexivity in reporting the experience of violence does not make a perfect match for judicial practice, especially in the case of women's experiences of violence within intimate relationships. Indeed, an *excess* of subjectivity, agency, and intentionality poses a problem to testimony in court, risking its becoming unpersuasive. At the same time, however, this excess makes it possible to disrupt the very logic entailed in truth-telling and in testimony on experiences of violence.

CHAPTER FOUR

The Gender of True-Lying

The site occupied by woman, by the lower classes, by the masses is that of excess; [... W]hat can be known about the feminized "object"? The answer to this question is "nothing" if we insist that this object is a pure phenomenon, a pure existence. However, if this object is indeed a social *object which is by nature "ridden with error" then criticizing it from within would amount to criticizing the social sources of its formation.*
Rey Chow, 1992

There is a kind of refusal to serve power that isn't a revolt or a rebellion but a revolution in the sense of reversing meanings, of changing how things are understood.
Ursula K. Le Guin, 2012

The Burden of Persuasion: Intention and Biased Evidence

The testimony of intimate violence victims in court relies on the request to speak in the absence of evidence, or rather, to produce a narrative about themselves providing all of the elements for judgment. As mentioned in Chapter Two, the Rocco Code and the Italian legal culture based on it assume a lack in female subjectivity that the institution has to fill. The mandatory rule clearly states that the law knows better than battered women do. Due to judgments in the wider society, their economic and social dependency, and their physical and psychological subjection, women are considered to be too much under social pressure to be able to tell the truth and stand firm. The judge is therefore tasked with interpreting the victim's socially induced lack of willingness to speak, and her true will. Women who are victims of violence at the hands of their partners are opaque: their interiority must be laid out in court in such a way that judges can take responsibility for it. In the dynamics of testifying in trials on domestic violence, the victims are pulled into a game of truth and power, in which both subjection and subjectivation are produced through varying forms of veridiction. The testimonies follow the path dictated by the requirements of the charge—to speak out—where the charge is the first step towards the formation of a complete, modern, rational, coherent, and disciplined subject. The normativity of the requests the justice system makes of female victims of intimate partner violence is caught up with the device of confession, which is aimed at producing a subjectivity capable of making sense of (and thus of granting transparency to) the actions submitted for judgment. The victim's own relation with her experience—that is, her capacity as a knower of it—is inextricably bound up with the persuasive power of her testimony. The authenticity of the narrated experience is central to the burden of persuading the court of the truth of violence, and thus, to producing evidence. The production of evidence hinges on a woman's testimony as to her experience of violence, which is in turn linked to the construction of a specific subjectivity. At the same time, the production of this persuasive subject is marked by the intersection of intentionality, agency, and deception. Excessively self-confident testimony has the potential to act against the victim.

An example of the issue of considering a victim's subjectivity can be drawn from work by Ong (2003).

Describing processes that build gendered citizenship in the United States among refugee communities, Ong addresses the complex relations between feminist empowerment and responses institutions give to acts of domestic violence. Ong poignantly illustrates a white, middle class, feminist, pastoral power, and the ways feminizing technologies shape minority subjectivity. Compassionate, patronizing, and racist stances towards Cambodian refugees, identified as backward and patriarchal, can be seen as social workers seek to empower women and urge them to leave their abusive partners, classifying dominant subjects by contrast with victims of patriarchy. Ong identifies a female subject, ethnically defined through customary family norms that are cast as expressions of unchallenged male power, who manages strategically, for her own ends, the logics of American social assistance. At play here is the truth of the couple relationship. The collapse of the intimate sphere, through the intervention of social services, creates ethnicized men on the one side and essentialized women victims as recipients of new rights on the other. If Ong calls attention to the perverse role of state logics that exacerbate family tensions, nonetheless we may wonder: could the fact that men are punished for behavior construed as resulting from ethnic patriarchy actually shift attention away from the violence that is exerted, and the fact that women may wish to escape from it? Can a "shrewd woman who expertly used social workers, the police, the court system, and the self-help group to turn things in her favor," against a disempowered, desperate husband (Ong 2003: 164) be a recognizable victim of domestic violence? Can her efforts to use the law to "punish and discipline" her partner, and sometimes even operate "mainly in her own self-interest," despite the "moral costs" to her family and community (2003: 166), mean a wish not so much to dominate her husband as to live a *different* intimacy, distant from menace and the constant threat of violence? What can be known of her choices, desires, and strategies, as ambivalent and disruptive as they appear? Moreover, can a victim be strategic?

A recurring element in my interviews with professionals was the need to dispel suspicion or doubt that a woman might be pressing charges for reasons of manipulation only. This concern plays a primary role in the progression of a trial. A contiguous significance is attributed to the victim's capacity for judgment, her awareness of the consequences, and a possible *manipulation* of her testimony. A woman who demands nothing, no sentence or compensatory damages, is perceived more positively, and positioned in a clear, indisputable juridical frame. As a woman prosecutor said revealingly during an interview,

> A woman who in some way [...] does not actively participate in the proceedings, the fact that this woman does not ask for compensatory damages, doesn't go to a lawyer and express in this way, impulsively, what happened, is judged positively as an element of reliability, period. [...] Because what needs to be excluded is the possibility of a personal interest, the injured party is not an indifferent witness, she is an interested witness because she could file a civil suit, she could successfully sue for damages and so you have to clear the air of the idea that there is a way to obtain something, to pursue personal interests beyond the simple desire to get to the truth of the matter [...] Paradoxically, if it happens that the injured party is very accurate, specific and meticulous, you have to exclude the possibility that there is some manipulative intent behind it to obtain damages, and so if a woman spontaneously presses charges and narrates a series of events and then stops collaborating, she becomes more reliable, because you understand that there are no interests behind it except telling what happened.[1]

1. Interview with female public prosecutor, Office of Procura, Bologna, April 2011.

This view is confirmed by conversations I observed between civil lawyers in the women's shelter, together with the interviews and informal communications that I had with them during my research. Judges often view the issue of spousal conflict—and how spouses make recourse to civil procedures at the same time as a criminal trial—almost as an *interference* in the normal victim-culprit sphere of domestic violence. In theory, civil and penal authorities should not know the issues in each other's respective trials. Nevertheless, whenever a trial takes place in civil court involving separation or the custody of minors, the defendant's lawyers inform the penal judge. In less serious cases, the act of pressing charges is considered to represent a bargaining chip in the woman's interactions with her partner, aimed at seeking custody of children or financial support after divorce. In this case, it is the woman's very efforts to claim her own legal rights that appears to be put on trial. This idea of a potentially manipulative intent behind charges also emerges in interviews conducted with judges. They clearly explain that, while a simultaneous civil dispute should not touch on a criminal trial in any way, in fact it can significantly affect the outcome of the proceedings.[2] The woman on the witness stand during the trial is seen as a potential liar, a bogus victim who lies in order to access certain rights, such as custody or compensatory damages, or simply for revenge. As Nader (2002) notes, in relation to mandatory mediation as an agent of control, the anger that can emerge in the legal process plays against abused women.[3] During a hearing in which the woman's testimony was focused on exonerating her husband of all charges, her

2. It is seldom the other way round, as civil procedures are definitely faster than penal ones.
3. In analyzing the language of the universal culture of negotiation and harmony ideology used to settle disputes that do not specifically have anything to do with the dimension of intimacy, Nader makes the point that this ideology is based

reliability as a witness was construed through the way that her own words cleared her ex-partner:

Defence: Have any other of his relatives ever beaten you up?
Witness: Once my father-in-law threatened me with a knife and my husband defended me. Then when I was pregnant with my second child he pushed me and so I lost the child.
D: And why would he push you?
Judge: I don't think that question is admissible…
D: To test the reliability of the witness!
J: It seems to me that the witness has shown herself to be very reliable, given her last declarations, which were very favorable to the accused.[4]

In light of this, any further step up the ladder of requests and demands paints the victim as an agent with the ability to act in her own interests, which actually works to undermine the *good* features of her femininity: sacrifice and candor. In other words, the charges must be detailed but not too detailed, lest they raise suspicions of manipulative intent on the woman's part. Since the truthfulness of the victim's testimony is of primary interest in investigations, any manipulative intention must be removed. In the words of the public prosecutor just quoted, what is decisive is the awareness of what is relevant for the law:

> It is easier to have an injured party who is aware of her situation, who understands exactly what you need to know and who is able to adequately represent the facts to you. If you have an injured party who doesn't realize that, who doesn't understand what is of interest, she might get caught up in more marginal questions. They tell you, for instance, more about problems with money

---

on a psychotherapeutic matrix and the rhetoric of "marital therapy" (Nader 2002: 155).

4. Field notes, October 18, 2010.

> than others... Because for these people paradoxically it is worse to struggle to make ends meet than to get slapped around at dinner, so if you are facing someone who has more tools and is able to provide a representation of reality that you find more adequate, it makes it easier for you to understand what all is about. The parties who are less aware, both in understanding what situation is victimizing them and what is actually important, make your so-to-speak "trial life" more difficult.

However, this awareness demanded of the woman is also the source of suspicion regarding the level of her agency: the subject is seen to exhibit a kind of behavior not appropriate for a victim, rendering her insufficiently victim-like. The law demands aware and emancipated subjects, but it also works to produce the subjectivity of the victim through invitations to express her persona and describe her behavior and emotional life. In the familial abuse context, the verification of violence brings together issues of love, relationship, family, reproduction, intimacy, desire, and sexuality: exemplary sites of the true self in a regime of truth. And yet, this true self is also suspected of bearing manipulative intent or an excess of awareness. The subject must be subjugated, passive, and aware, all at the same time. In most cases, the victim fails to stage this performance of an (adequate) inner being, or does so only partially, thus coming off as either absent or excessively agentive. Men's intentions in using violence are not of interest to the court: any motivation given by the defense as justification is rejected as illegitimate by the judges. Intention and interiority are at stake only for the victim. The same public prosecutor continues with how this interior should be evident through clues in the victim's communicative style, such as that the "appropriate emotional tone" be evident in the delivery:

> So, the abuser says "It's not true, I've never raised a hand," and you might have medical reports stating that

> something might have happened, or even without the reports, because it's not guaranteed that the injured party went to the hospital, but anyway you always have the statements of an injured party which, if they pass an extremely in-depth evaluation of their intrinsic and extrinsic reliability, that is, if the statements are logical, accurate, noncontradictory, if they have an appropriate emotional tone or are delivered in such a way as to not present elements casting doubt on their reliability, these alone can constitute the basis of a conviction.

Agency vs Credibility

How persuasive is a story of a relationship that features the victim's inability to understand her condition as being subjugated, casting her as lacking awareness? Or does she rather demonstrate awareness, but with a manipulative intent? In what sense can such testimony be evidence? And how is it related to persuasion? As described in Chapter Three, the burden of proof lies in the production of evidence, and, at the same time, in persuading the judges that facts alleged are true. Hastrup (2004), reflecting on evidence, has suggested that anthropological knowledge challenges a defining (if implicit) property of evidence, because it conveys the excess of the meaning of social experience through ethnography. The assumed property of evidence is to be free of human intention, such that the seeming fabrication of evidence disqualifies it as such (Hastrup 2004: 460). As historian of science Lorraine Daston, quoted in Hastrup, maintains: "[T]he blood-stained weapon found at the scene of a murder counts as evidence as long as it was not planted there with the intention of incriminating; the *unaffected simplicity* of the witness adds weight to testimony as long as it was not feigned with the intention of persuading" (Daston 1994: 244; my italics). Hastrup brilliantly comments on this observation to discuss the ways in which science and statistics rely upon processes of categorization entangled in intentionality. I would further stress how ethnography can question the perspective of the witness on this notion of what evidence entails, and the ambiguous role of intentionality found in legal reasoning. Daston's wording provides two quite different pictures. The first involves the obvious manipulation of evidence, while the other is testimony directed at persuading, which is technically legitimate. The fact that the judge easily sees through it, and recognizes it as contrived, might mean that the account has been dramatized badly, but it tells us nothing about the veracity of the facts to be ascertained. Detecting an intent to persuade immediately implies judgment about intentions. The factor that causes problems here is the added weight of "unaffected simplicity" in judgments concerning testimony that is caught up in webs of ambivalence, as is testimony about domestic violence. What is judged is the act of testifying, more than the given content of the statements, which cannot be objectified as evidence.

Testimonial evidence is delivered in a framework that makes it accusatory all by itself, and yet at the same time implies that it cannot be too precise or too *intentional* to be considered true, and thus to count as evidence. To generate evidence, persuasive testimony must be spontaneous, of the kind Daston (1994: 244) likens to "nature's facts." Testimony that is too precise, too emotional, or not emotional enough, fails to constitute evidence. Where the issue of agency and style turns out to be crucial, this duality to the testimony of women—at once natural victims and manipulators—is part of a cultural climate that has historically produced the female subject in an ambivalent way. The gendered dimension thus calls into question intentionality as an element of legal evidence. The relationship between persuasion and evidence enables the investigation of the authentic/inauthentic, affected/unaffected dynamic in the legal and social management of domestic violence. Indeed, the suitable victim-subject is one who, free of demands or claims, does not *seek* to demonstrate that she is a victim, but *shows* herself to be one authentically and naturally. The narrative demanded by the court must meet certain criteria of credibility: it must have the right "emotional tone" when recounting the violence in question. Asked about the possibility of allowing a woman plaintiff to use a cover in order to feel more at ease while testifying, the judge who ruminated above on inner conviction expressed reservations:

> These are measures taken in exceptional cases because, in the end, it is very important that the defendant's lawyer—while examining a witness, whatever witness—can watch her reactions beyond her words; in many cases it does not matter as much what the witness says, but mostly what she does while talking to a lawyer, and so it is important to see her.[5]

The testimony is judged on a performative style that turns suffering into experience, that expresses desires for justice but not for revenge, and that speaks, forcing its way past a victim's natural silence. Any expressions of anger or excessive emotion are signs that she is faking and thus unreliable. Testimony must be persuasive but not intentional, not manufactured; in a word, it must be authentic. An authentic victim is one who hesitates as such. Ultimately, the confessional apparatus to which she is subjected during the trial, in the place of the absent perpetrator, enacts that specific kind of ritual "in which the truth is corroborated by the obstacles and resistances it has to surmount in order to be formulated" (Foucault 1978: 61-62). In the absence of evidence of bodily injuries, the court seeks to identify

5. Interview with female judge, Office of Criminal Court, Bologna, March 2011. During the court hearings I observed, the defendant, when present, often sat next to his lawyer, in the front row, very close to the witness.

wounds of the soul, eliciting the testimony of the plaintiff as victim that coincides with her inability to take action: "Did she still love him?" In domestic violence hearings, the most authentic testimonies—where the fact that the account is unaffected and impartial is taken to mean that it is genuine—are very close to silence. It is the relationship between speech and silence that produces the evidence of wounded intimacy, painting the picture of an interior world that is worthy. Just as in the refugee testimonies discussed above, it is far from plain how to interpret and report the witnesses' voices and what they convey (Cabot 2016). If the problem of evidence is essentially a problem of speech in relation to experience (Csordas 2004: 479), interpreting silence is complicated in criminal law, as its meaning can include diverse and even opposing reasons: trauma, second thoughts, the effects of threats, a non-cooperative stance, distrust in the law itself.

A woman who has suffered violence is thus by definition unable to speak: her voice is determined by the power that dominates her, and therefore is not authoritative. However, for its correct functioning, the institutional dimension requires the victim to be conscious of her situation. If she were not conscious, she would not be able to speak. Only a conscious and emancipated subject can have recourse to the law. Paradoxically, adhering to this demand distances the woman who speaks from the victim-subject: from the moment she decides to speak, she is no longer a victim. In this respect, evidence and persuasion are clearly in a relationship of contradiction. On the one hand, social services and national campaigns insist on the need to press charges and to take a public stance against violence endured. On the other hand, the court's tendency to interpret the intentionality of the victim's testimony as artifice and seduction—indeed, the very fact that she speaks out—prevents the testimony from being persuasive. The victim who declares herself, who claims to have been wronged, becomes something else: a conscious subject and thus an agent, who automatically renders herself less identifiable as a victim. The confessional device produces an individual detached from her own categorization: "While avowal ties the subject to what he affirms, it also qualifies him differently with regard to what he says: criminal, but perhaps susceptible to repent; in love, but it has now been declared; ill, but already conscious and detached enough from his illness that he himself can work toward his own healing" (Foucault 2014: 17).

The intention of the victim is thus what is put on trial in various mutually contradictory ways. The first of these is the requirement that she not be manipulative, and therefore that she present herself in court as a victim: a lack of intentionality as evidence. The second has to do with intentionality as a dimension of the kind of self-reflexivity and awareness that defines the emergence of a subject and her ability to speak for herself: intentionality as a prerequisite for credibility when taking the stand, which is an element of the legal illocutionary act. The third involves awareness as a space for manipulation or demanding reparations for a wrong: the gendered excess of intentionality that is taken to indicate seduction. Italian jurisprudence shares a rhetoric that is rampant in the peculiar context of contemporary Italian society, where women's voices are marginalized or captured within conservative frames. As women respond to demands to speak the violence, their victimhood is therefore compromised. This is an imaginary conditioned by historical prejudices about greedy and aggressive femininity, focused on women's seductive and manipulative capacities, and also by the image of the *genuinely* passive victim of violence, a caring and self-sacrificing figure who seeks nothing for herself.

The law of procedure involves judges putting aside what common sense tells them. They must see and listen to what they are being shown during the trial, but avert their gaze from the context, which they must ignore. Otherwise, they jeopardize their capacity for judgment (Garapon 1997: 314). Letting oneself be persuaded by a woman's account involves a risk: if she is not a real victim, her account will instead be characterized by seduction. The women's shelter lawyers who work on domestic violence explicitly discuss the issue of whether or not to suggest that victims dress 'appropriately' (not too seductively) when testifying in court. The off-scene question frequently posed at hearings—"Did you still love him?"—is linked to the peculiar ambiguity of intimacy itself, representing the truest dimension of the individual and yet that which is most vulnerable to the proof of authenticity. Intimacy immediately entails questions of pretention and performance:

> 'Is s/he genuine? Or is s/he faking it?' The expression of intimacy is guided by cultural codes, what ought to be hidden and what ought to be revealed, how intimacy should be performed or expressed. (Sehlikoglu and Zengin 2015: 23)

In the Italian courts, this expression of an intimate relationship, of betrayed love and experiences of pain and violence, is expected to conform to a specific code which stems from a cultural understanding of the gendered self. Hearings on domestic violence are spaces where the intimate dimension is subjected to careful scrutiny. At the same time, however, the very fact that this intimacy must be revealed means that it cannot be shown without the loss of its defining characteristic, namely its inexpressibility: "What kinds of discrepancies, vulnerabilities and even ferocities are created, then, when the sincerity of intimacy is questioned by third parties, state officers and others?" (Sehlikoglu and Zengin 2015: 23).

In this context, the longstanding depiction of women as cunning and masked subjects intersects with the fictive character of the law. The woman who speaks at a domestic violence trial is not so much communicating evidence of the facts as she is communicating the fact that she tells the truth. Her credibility turns on a performative act concerning her own intimacy, her experience of suffering, and this already constitutes a suspicious element in and of itself when it is enacted on a legal stage. At the same time, the performance of detachment from which the court derives its authority (Latour 2010) is particularly frail. As reported by the judges themselves, the process of formulating a verdict is rendered difficult by the slipperiness of the issue—it is domestic, familiar, personal, relational: in a word, intimate. The judge lacks sufficient distance: "All of us are judges, men, women, fathers, mothers, sons. This entails a risk ... it always involves a susceptibility to getting pulled into the matter, on a human level."[6]. Investigated in stories and in subjects that speak of violence, but necessarily removed in the creation of judgment, intimacy creates an impermeable sheath that remains constitutively separate from the events. This subject that fails to stage her interiority as requested, to conform to the subject-function of the judicial system, this *remainder* of the judicial scene, this incongruous subject that represents a problem for the execution of justice, remains largely unexplored. Beginning precisely from this incongruity, however, possibilities for action can be uncovered that take unpredictable forms and play an important role in repositioning the victim-subject of domestic violence.

Conley and O'Barr note that "the burden of stylistic powerlessness, which falls most heavily on women, minorities, poor, uneducated, is compounded on the discourse level by the tendency among the same groups to organize their legal arguments around concerns that the courts are likely to treat as irrelevant" (1990: 81). The process of ascertaining the truthfulness of a victim's testimony is the lynchpin from which the dynamics of trial unfold. Prosecutors and judges assess the credibility of testimony through judgments that are closely tied to assumptions about gender: assumptions which themselves contain

6. Interview with male public prosecutor, Office of Procura, Bologna, May 2011.

assessments of personality. At play here is that figure often encountered in an Italian imaginary fueled by Catholicism: the woman-mother, vestal of the family, a figure governed by specific norms and oriented toward providing care, and characterized by modesty and sacrifice (D'Amelia 2005). The feminine experience envisioned as a space of dignity through sacrifice for family makes the white Italian woman an allegorical figure who must speak in order to give voice to the future of the nation, its reproductive continuity. The notion of *decoro* (decency, propriety, deservingness) is a powerful tool for defining the authority of the female voice (Gribaldo 2018), and for keeping at bay those who cannot afford individual affirmation—that is, *freedom*—in the face of current political and economic crises (Pitch 2013). There are multiple elements relevant to this context: a removal from collective memory of the experience of migration, within and beyond national borders; the constant banalization of episodes of racism; and the nationalist rhetoric and laws on immigration that have emerged even on the occasion of the recent anniversary of the unification of Italy (Boni 2012). Public discourses on the fate of the nation identify women as guardians of national values (Gissi 2010). What social service managers in Bologna call 'cultural' dynamics, in cases involving immigrants, is no different from what is found in cases that include Italian women as protagonists. In the discourse of social workers and legal professionals, the behavior and attitudes of people from other countries are judged through a generic ethno-cultural classification that associates culture with race. In hearings I witnessed, legal workers used phrases such as "the foreign witness" or "the Moroccan accused" on more than one occasion, with the justification that non-Italian names are hard to pronounce. In the courtroom, some immigrant women use stereotypical notions of "European culture," construed as having achieved full gender equality, in claims against their foreign husbands: something that I never observed in interviews. This mimics interpretations of their own cultural backgrounds, as inexorably sexist and violent, that are widespread in the host community. In one case, a Muslim woman who was testifying to violence had to listen to a closing statement where the public prosecutor described her and her partner as belonging to "a culture where women are considered a sub-species to subjugate and degrade."[7] In another case, a woman made recourse to self-stereotyping in order to convince the court: "[I said to my husband], we are in Europe, not in Africa in the middle of the jungle."[8] The use of this reference is evidently instrumental for the witness. She did not consider the context to be pervasive: she maintained that she had had a happy childhood, and that her husband's attitude was due to his having been beaten as a child. Indeed, at one point she turned the defense accusation against her culture of origin into an accusation against her husband's family instead:

Defence: How come he behaved like this? I want to better understand the reasons.
Witness: He wanted to be right about everything.
D: Was it his culture that led him to act like this?
W: In his family, the women had to wash the dishes, I don't agree with that.
D: It didn't happen for no reason then…
W: Of course not, he isn't mad!

The reference to culture can also be used to justify the behavior of the husband. It was unsurprisingly used by the defense in the final discussion of this same case, on the grounds that, from the moment a woman is Westernized, she can no longer be a victim:

> Let's say that his behavior is clearly not that of a gentleman, but since the wife denounced him and told

7. Field notes, February 7, 2011.
8. Field notes, December 12, 2010.

> her husband straight away, it makes you think that the wife has adopted a Western mentality and is very proud of that, but this also means that she is not scared, that actually all this dominance doesn't exist.

Once you speak as a Westerner, you are no longer a dominated person; you can no longer be afraid, since race and gender as conditions of subalternity are viewed as a personal sediment in the liberal, plural, culturally different individual (Greenhouse 2017). Prejudices can also play a role when police receive pleas from foreign women to charge their partners. Some workers from the shelter suggested that such women are more readily believed if the man in question is considered to be from a sexist cultural background. Racist discourses in Italy are part of a longstanding model that targets the Southern Italian working class (Schneider 1998). It is therefore no surprise that this cultural logic is applied to Southern Italian men as well: "The Carabinieri were very understanding. My ex-partner is from Naples, and they said, 'Look, it's not the first time that this has happened to us [...] the culture is like that over there.'"[9]

All of these testimonies—those that tell stories about relationships and about all kinds of violence; those that are silent and evasive; those that are confused; those cut short by using stereotypes as a stratagem—are varying responses to the prompt to "Tell me who you are."

Oblique Narratives: The Imperfect Victim

Various recent studies have reflected on different ways of speaking the truth, of expressing subjectivity in unexpected ways, while giving examples of the co-constitution of subjection and subjectivation, and problematizing the

9. Interview with Bruna, Casa delle donne, Bologna, December 2010.

notion of resistance. Anthropologists engaging with post-structuralist and feminist understandings of subjectivity and resistance have widened the scope for finding agency in contexts where subjectivity does not imply this remainder, where the direction that corrodes the norm is not necessarily foreseen. In dialogue with Butler, Mahmood (2005) suggests we do away with the remnants of a liberal conception of autonomy, in order to give us space to reconsider unexpected forms of being, and practices that do not fit into narratives of subversion. Her work on the subjectivity of Cairene women involved in the movement for moral reform explodes the schema of liberty and oppression, where the former is supposed to coincide with self-expression, and the latter with the alienation of will. Mahmood especially underlines how Butler's Foucauldian understanding of the subject—whose autonomy and self-consciousness is created through the same processes that secure its subordination—implies a concept of agency that exposes norms to resignification within an agonistic structure enacting or subverting them (2005: 22). She rethinks the notion of practices of resistance outside a predetermined framework that refers to a teleology of progressive politics and that focuses on the subversion of norms through iteration and performativity. Her ethnography confronts practices that are indifferent to the goal of subversion but nonetheless express self-realization and self-transformation, challenging the conception of autonomy and freedom as normatively liberatory. The very notion of agency appears as released from a series of implicit links with the field of autonomy and resistance. Mahmood considers specific dispositions that coordinate inner states and outer conducts by returning to Foucault, and particularly to his work on ethics and practices of care of the self that transform the subject in order to achieve a state of truth.

The issue of structure and freedom is crucial to an anthropology of ethics. Here I wish to linger on one aspect of Foucault's thought, on the ethics of *parrhesia*—

the act of telling all, plain speaking, frank speech—as a premise of ethical conduct. Found in Foucault's late works, this is a starting point for reflecting on ways of acting on and responding to the implacability of disciplinary and institutional devices. Here an active subject appears, partially contrasting with the previous theorizations of the subject that he elaborated within the framework of power-knowledge. Focusing on freedom as an aspect of power relations, and on a more affirmative relation to truth, Foucault's late reflections insist upon the transformative force of experience, and on truth-telling as a criticism of the powers that be. At the core of these reflections on parrhesia lies a specific type of relationship between speakers and what they say, and the antinomian power that certain words in certain circumstances might produce. What is crucial for my argument is that the radical alterity of the parrhesiastes is due to the use of speaking; to the concrete ways that the act of speaking marks a new subjectivity. This subject proves the truth not so much by evidence or argument, but rather by the act of speaking out. The outcomes are, moreover, not forecast. The act does not have codified effects, and its effects are unexpected (Foucault 2010: 62). The notion of parrhesia as it is introduced by Foucault, in particular when he analyses Euripides' *Ion*, is deeply gendered. The possibility of identifying a woman as a parrhesiastes is marked by the peculiarity of her condition. Creusa, the princess of Athens who gives birth to Ion after she is raped by Apollo, is an unusual parrhesiastes because she accuses power and at the same time confesses the truth regarding herself. Her modes of expression are "confession-imprecation" and "confession-confidence" (Foucault 2010: 139). Her speaking is personal, not political. She tells the truth, but she lacks self-control and specific intentionality, since she speaks in her anger (Foucault 2010: 108; Maxwell 2018). Foucault draws attention to the ambiguity of value in the idea of a parrhesia that oscillates between the courage to speak the truth and the anarchic indiscrete "chattering about anything concerning oneself" (2010: 47). Feminist reflections claim this very same ambiguity: the necessity to use and at the same time never completely adhere to an institutionalized political language. That which we 'cannot not want' makes us subaltern, but it also allows us to claim. From this tangle emerges the need to consider hesitations, and the unexpectedly oblique and mediating modes of testimony, action, subtraction, and resistance.

Anthropology might indeed consider silences and elisions that take place in the everyday. Terms such as agency and intentionality hardly lend themselves to the analysis of dynamics in the expression of intimate violence (Das 2007). The possibilities of witnessing can be diverse, and each is related to a specific time and space. An anthropology of hesitations might offer a chance to consider expressions and stances exceeding the framework of agency that conflates them with ambivalence or reticence. Limited to the legal frame, my ethnographic work here intends to make visible and explore dynamics in court. These are in some ways very predictable. That women are not believed, as long asserted by feminists, is increasingly being recognized by professionals, and more generally in public discourse. Nonetheless, this awareness is marked by the difficulty of making it a truly political issue. Perhaps this is exactly because it belongs to the already known, the everyday, the expected. The complexity of testifying, of expressing *témoignage,* permits an ethnographic investigation of the production of difference, the remainder between the subject and the power that creates it. By looking at how migrants in detention centers express themselves through their bodies, in self-directed violence, Banu Bargu (2017) investigates the nature of agency in truth-telling acts. The undecidability of the outcome of extreme protest actions calls into question the notion that action is simply a means to an end. Comprising radical practices of the self and the expressive forms that manifest them, this parrhesia of the weak contests the concept of the political itself. It questions the understanding of resistance as linked to claims for rights or recognition. The very irruption of testimony likewise has a political power, as much as the subtraction that responds to institutional demands. Heath Cabot (2016) has discussed how it is impossible to investigate personal story or intention in the case of a woman fleeing her country of origin. The woman's refusal to speak when accessing services in the host country questions practices of knowledge in anthropology and in advocacy. Her sabotage of the structures of power in which she is caught refracts the violence of any effort to know the subject, to know her motivations and inner intentions. But a ghostly presence remains.

These are examples where individuals called on to represent themselves and their conditions, in a framework that over-determines them, express something different to what is expected: a challenge, a subtraction, a swerve. Different expressions of inner states manifest differently. From the individual who speaks of intimate partner violence, the law requires congruence, accountability, and intentionality. It asks for a statement. Yet the modes of expression sometimes render something else, beyond the intentionality of assertion or the idioms of agency, resilience, and resistance. They sometimes render a different way of being. Parrhesia is not necessary linked to logos, as it "may appear in the things themselves, it may appear in ways of doing things, it may appear in ways of being" (Foucault 2010: 320). According to Foucault, what is at stake is not the autonomy of the subject but the very possibility of being. Political agency is rethought in the examples above, along with the idea of the intentional subject. The desire to get closer to a model of pious self, to protest under oppressive circumstances, to disappear from institutions, exceeds the potentialities of normative action. In the case of domestic violence, exceedingly expressive modes of testimony and the lack of a clear-cut intention—to stick to social services, to leave the abuser, to tell the truth to institutions, to seize the law—challenge a justice system that would attach to intention the notions of claim, accountability, and credibility.

Here I wish to linger on one case in which a woman's behavior in court—her self-expression, and references that brought race, gender, and class into play—were so evidently performative as to produce an eccentric response to the court's demands. This case illustrates an intertwining of issues that the parties involved were constantly re-invoking and re-triggering. In this trial the accused was a man from Albania. Giovanna, the injured party who was pressing charges for battery and threats, and filing for damages, had Sicilian origins. She had sole custody of their two children. Around forty, Giovanna appeared in the courtroom looking determined and at ease, youthful, with blond highlights in her hair. A long shirt over her wide hips displayed a woman's face and the words "love is glamorous," over jeans and a striking white pair of high heels. During the three hours of proceedings, issues of a cultural and racial nature were frequently invoked. An interweaving of stereotypes was evident, in addition to assumptions regarding gender, which complicated the case. Both witnesses and the defense, who had a strong Southern Italian accent, constantly referenced the woman's Southern origins to explain her behavior. The neighbors testified that the woman was a *terrona* (an insulting term for a Southerner) and did not speak Italian but *maruchen* (literally "Moroccan": an offensive term used in the dialect of the Emilia-Romagna region to indicate Southern dialects). The judge, a woman, intervened in the exchanges in order to clarify and to make comments, sometimes ironically:

Defence: [*Addressing an elderly woman neighbor who testifies for the defense*] Were you ever present during the arguments?
Witness: No, never. I heard her shouting all the time. I didn't understand anything because she speaks foreign, Moroccan dialect.
Judge: [*Smiling*] By Moroccan, you mean a dialect from the southern part of Italy.

W: I don't even know where she comes from.
[...]
The woman's husband, born in Palermo, comes in to testify. The judge, hearing his origins, intervenes.
J: Therefore you are someone who speaks Moroccan out of need! As your wife says... [*The man looks around, perplexed.*] It was a joke because it often happens in mixed marriages; I have a vague personal experience...[10]

Giovanna accused the defendant of having used his clearly dangerous "Albanian friends" to threaten her. The defense claimed that the woman had made racist comments about the man, defining him and his family as "dirty Albanians" and "gypsies." The defense described the injured party as an ignorant Southern Italian woman who did not conform to parameters of distinction proper to middle-class behavior: she shouted, spoke in dialect, yelled at her children; she was "noisy" and lacked refinement; her job as a secretary was sporadic and unreliable; her cultural and professional competences were judged laughable. (Indeed, her self-presentation provoked frequent laughter during the hearing.) Repeated references were made to her troubled familial past, to the two children that she had from a prior relationship. Giovanna's manner in the courtroom also clashed powerfully with the model of coherence, calm, and clarity required by the judges and the court. Rather than the "appropriate emotional tone" that would have made her appear neither too much the victim nor too much the agent, her testimony slid into the realm of excess. Her narrative was peculiar. It displayed a marked self-confidence and nonchalance, in sharp contrast to the pattern that hearings usually see, of absences, silences, tears, embarrassment, and fragmented speech interrupted by emotional outbursts. It was clear that she had a low level of formal education, and a poor mastery of Italian. She had trouble reading the oath,

10. Field notes, October 21, 2010.

and her testimony was full of syntactic and grammatical errors, alongside bits of dialect. During the trial she did not understand—or pretended not to understand—requests for clarification. She did not acknowledge having contradicted herself, and she failed to present a chronological account of events. Her behavior also departed from normal protocols of appropriate interaction. She commented on statements from the prosecutor and judge by saying "Brava" (essentially, "Good girl"), to mean "Correct." She interrupted them while they were speaking, and even spoke out of turn, often drowning out the questions she was being asked with her own words. Although the judge tried to keep her in check—"Don't make comments about what I say!"—exchanges with the defense and public prosecutor often ended in overlapping speech, and requests for clarification were ignored.

Giovanna's self-expression evoked an element of popular Mediterranean and Southern Italian culture: *la piazzata*, or quarreling in raised voices out in the open, often on balconies extending over the street, with meaningful gestures, innuendos, and humorous quips, often unmasking hypocrisy (De Filippo 1964; Busatta 2006). This expressive mode has been revisited by popular television shows in which quarrels are publicly staged in front of an audience, mediated by the day's host.[11] Given how popular culture and the media forge visions of the self, Giovanna realistically reproduced and acted out television-style scenes of self-representation in terms of domestic conflict. She asserted incoherence in the face of the requirements of the criminal justice system, claiming the chance to publicly narrate her own experience of violence without conforming to the canons of authenticity required of intimate partner violence victims. Her behavior ranged from displays of irony,

11. Television shows bringing on separated couples include *C'eravamo tanto amati* (We used to love each other so much) and *Arrivederci amore ciao* (Goodbye my love, bye bye).

heedless of contradictions, to unscrupulous stereotyping and self-stereotyping, as well as putting the judge in the role of managing the debate, as if she were a TV host with a role confined to commenting on the representation offered. Italian television has produced multiple programs for women that stage gendered styles of communication in very obvious ways. The presence of a woman host in entertainment programs that are designed for a female audience establishes a discursive space that revolves around introspection and psychological insight. The host becomes a detective tasked with exploring existential pathways, and asking guests to clarify statements they made about themselves in other occasions. Here, "female skills, whether applied to the hosting of the program or displayed by the guests, always end up reduced to the sphere of managing intimacy and feelings" (Demaria 2003: 206; my translation). As an imperfect victim, Giovanna displayed dimensions of eccentricity that disrupted the dominant framework wherein the victim is only allowed to reproduce herself and remains trapped by the impossible, contradictory demands of the juridical apparatus.

Gender, race, culture, and class are elements "most often treated in mainstream liberal discourse as vestiges of bias or domination" (Crenshaw 1994: 93; see Connell 1997). The peculiarity of Giovanna's case is that extra-juridical issues focus on ethnic and social background. Gender and intimacy are brought into play and deployed, rupturing the category of the perfect victim-subject. This way, the behavioral traits associated with the much-discussed battered-woman syndrome and its "learned helplessness"[12] (Walker 2000), along with the stereotypes that work to produce credibility and appropriateness in the testifying

12. This refers to a psychological theory that identifies a "cycle of abuse" involving three phases—"tension-building," "acute battering incident," and a "honeymoon,"—as the reason for the return of battered women to abusive relationships.

subject, sometimes come to be inverted, re-interpreted, and overturned in obliquely oppositional ways. Giovanna's account, her unexpectedly frank speech that exceeded the pastoral exercise of confession, disrupted expectations of how the self should be narrated in the testimony of violence victims, disarticulating the mechanism that locates the victim's painful authenticity in her perceived credibility. In trial, the truthfulness of the suffering of the witness, taking on the character of a confession, is proven to be authentic by the obstacles or resistances that the subject must overcome to pronounce her account. In this case, it is precisely such resistance that the injured party negated. Renouncing modes of silence or hesitation that might act to confirm the truthfulness of her testimony, she refused to engage in identifying her true self in the ways the device of confession would demand.

Although the judge sought to contain Giovanna's expressions as much as possible, they nonetheless gave a character to the hearing. Displays of suffering in the expected emotional tone, and conformation with the woman-victim stereotype through the narrative of the subjugated subject, gave way instead to a dramatized scene that was aimed not so much at saying something different as at showing oneself and claiming to be something different from the role that women are asked to act out (White 1990). In an ethnography of the construction of credibility in testimony in Italian *camorra* (criminal society) trials, Marco Jacquemet (1996: 11) calls "communicative performance" the social practice of producing representations of the world and persuading others to comply with these representations. By escaping expected discursive and linguistic modes, Giovanna's use of expressive and performative forms from popular styles afforded her, if not quite the capacity to persuade, at least an unexpected repositioning. The gendered game of the parties to a domestic violence courtroom scene was subjected to the dynamics of an eccentric presentation.

Near the end of the trial, the female judge literally got up from her bench and moved closer to Giovanna to speak to her:

Judge: I am going to ask you some additional questions now, and please do not think that I seek to intrude in the intimate details of your life, seeing as these are such painful matters. You said that the relationship had finished in 2006 and you stopped living together. You sought and asked for reconciliation. Why did you do that? What were your reasons?
Giovanna: I still loved him.
J: I suspected that you were still in love…
G: And then I saw that the kids were crying.
J: When did you resign yourself?
G: After one year. And then, really, after four months, when he didn't give me spousal support or anything.
J: But was the reason your strong feelings or only the money?
G: My strong feelings, I was in love.
J: Good, we're finished here.

What happened in these last exchanges? What is the meaning of these last sentences, sliding as they do into the realm of emotions in order to conclude a long, fragmented hearing? The judge's words convert the classic question "Why didn't you leave him?" (which entails the pathologizing "Did you still love him despite the battering?"), into the empathic "Were you in love?" Her speech enacts a shift from the realm of action to that of emotion. The contextual dynamics, the diffuse perception of gender, the references to intimacy, mix with procedural logic in search of meaningful subjectivity. No longer central is the technique of imputation that requires every speech act to be traced back to its speaker. Publicly acknowledging that the neutrality of her ruling is a pretense (Berns 1999), the judge grants surprising meaningfulness to Giovanna's testimony. This exchange rests on the sharing of a gendered location deployed through the exhibition of intimacy. Action may be reconducted to a state of mind and heart that displays a gendered disposition towards love, care, sacrifice, and relation. The intention of accusing her partner is dissolved in this disposition. Without lingering on the issues raised here by the gender of the judge and legal professionals, and the different speech genres they might have employed, I emphasize that, to make a definitive ruling, the judge involved in this dismantling of the confessional device found herself, at the end of the trial, calling on the witness to certify the authenticity of her testimony. Giovanna fulfilled this request through a recognizable but contextually unexpected expression of self, a subjectivity expressed through her intimate relationship with the perpetrator. And yet the judge did not so much interrogate Giovanna as confirm what had become clear to her during the hearing through Giovanna's unorthodox testimony.

Diverse authors have investigated the issue of the suffering self, showing that "the capacity to notice and document suffering (even if it be one's own suffering) from the position of a generalized and necessarily disembodied observer is what marks the beginnings of the modern self" (Chakrabarty 2000: 119; see Boltanski 1993). Yet these unsettling modes of expression and their effects in institutional settings suggest a different view. The shift from the investigation of violent acts to investigating the victim's personal story and inner feelings, the move towards the expression of feelings as crucial and revelatory for judgment, highlights the intertwining of modernity, media culture, and the gendered self. Modernity as mass culture has historically been understood as feminine, in a devaluation associating women with the masses: degradation of taste, sentimentalization of culture, the association of high culture with masculinity and consumerism with femininity. Even in attempts to re-evaluate mass culture as potentially revolutionary, the notion of simulation has been linked with feminine seduction (Modleski 1991). Emphasizing how feminine mass culture is both public and private at the same time, Berlant (2008: 3) writes that "the intimate public legitimates qualities, ways of being, and entire lives that have otherwise been deemed puny or discarded. It creates situations where these qualities can appear as luminous."

Thus, the presentation of a suffering self, in unexpected ways that make the gendered subaltern subject recognizable, presents an implicit challenge to an institutional system that produces re-victimization. Women who take the stand at domestic abuse trials are called on to over-identify with painful experiences. Particular, physical, sayable violence: this is what makes them reliable victims. This comes as no surprise, given that legal intelligibility demands a process of classifying:

> The law's typical practice is to recognize kinds of subjects, acts and identities: it is to taxonomize. What is the relation between the (seemingly inevitable) authoritarianism of juridical categorization, and the other, looser spaces of social life and personhood that do not congeal in categories of power, cause, and effect the way the law does? (Berlant 1999: 75)

In the face of this hailing of the victim-subject, a figure that cannot be performed straightforwardly, is it possible to refuse the juridico-politics of affect that measures injustice by proving the feelings expressed, the experience of violence, and its suitable dramatization? Notions of victimhood, intimacy, experience, and gender shape the narratives of evidence. We may join Giordano (2015: 25) in wondering if it is possible to acknowledge the testimonies that emerge from the intersections of different truth regimes and truth demands, to recognize "a testimony that does not qualify as truthful but is nevertheless not a lie."

These practices recall what Agamben (2005) calls profanations. These open up the possibility of restoring to human practice that which had been relegated to a sacred and intangible sphere, thus refusing its confinement in the imaginary. Profanations cause the *dispositif* of confession to go round in circles, detaching it from an immediate end. The merging of life and politics, of what is incommunicable and not, provides the fragile possibility of a space for a language not finalized and not necessarily linked to a subject already defined by the law. Profanation in the contexts analyzed here relates to the unexpected ways that victims respond to the requirements of the law. Women must flirt with the demand of a complete adhesion to being themselves, speaking the truth in the most authentic way, thus dramatizing and acting out the intimate truth of partner violence. Sometimes these disruptions are enacted in ways that historically have been marginalized or captured by media culture, made unavailable to testify about anything. The dramatization of feelings, grievances, sudden silences, smirks, are all excesses ascribed to gendered and racialized modes of communication. Ethnography suggests that these modalities are produced through inadequate means, by subjects who are not foreseen, or conversely are too evident to be taken into account. The difference entailed in gender, class, and race is commonly recognized yet at the same time put on hold for being an obstacle to the smoothness of judgment. Nonetheless, these everyday profanations are never extraneous to the sinuous game entangling insidious prejudice with formalism. They can always be traced in the way that judgments are made (Latour 2010).

In this respect, true lying is the peculiar modality used by women who are victims of intimate partner violence, in order to report an intimate personal experience that is not supposed to be expressed, unless with manipulatory intentions. To tell a consequential story, to press charges, to denounce a violent partner, is required of a woman and yet at the same time cannot be expected if not as a fake. Stories of intimacy and everyday violence that do not conform to requirements of authenticity, that abound with ambiguities and complexities, do not constitutively exclude the possibility of appealing to different truths, of calling on judges' inner convictions and partially contradicting the indifference of their judgments. The specific forms of *dire vrai* allow the giving of meaning to a crime. In this way the extra-juridical establishes the juridical and at the same time puts it at risk. Such a judgment would not be based upon the details but, in moving away from norms about stating the facts, on a recognition that truth instead lies elsewhere: in the space of the context, in relationships of power between genders, in representations of intimacy and the relationship itself; in short, in that which cannot legitimately be investigated in the legal space.

Conclusions

The issue of domestic violence interrogates and is interrogated by different kinds of knowledge. Its tangle of gendered subjectivity, intimacy, and experience makes it elusive and at the same time already known, related to a private sphere of common knowledge. For this reason, it is difficult to capture in statistics, to analyze through the social sciences, to deal with in institutions, or to identify and judge before the law. In the context of debates about domestic violence, the injunction on the speaker and witness to self-identify is powerfully conditioned by a number of requirements revolving around her credibility. These range from the content of her testimony (coherent, detailed, quantitative), to her intentions (detached from specific contingencies), to the way that she expresses herself (a truthful tone appropriate to a victim-subject). This entanglement of factors makes it impossible for the testimony to hold legal significance, thus rendering it essentially lacking and inconsistent. The task of demonstrating violent acts in front of institutions is caught up in the same mechanisms of knowing and identification already tied to intimacy very closely. The facts in question enjoy a special status, in that a single speaking subject has to demonstrate them.

The testimonies of violence I have analyzed usually involve an experience reported by a single actor, the woman witness, formulated for a specific audience, subjected to judgment, and required to be persuasive. Nevertheless, the evidence cannot speak for itself, because it is forced through a subjectivity that does not meet socio-legal demands. The path to speaking out—through the interpellation of women to express themselves, by police, welfare services, the law, and society in general—involves an array of responses according to the institutions and individuals involved. Testimonies might be construed as emancipatory or manipulative, as related to responsibility or to potential civil claims. Opaque descriptions (what she really experienced), wavering determination (continuously filing charges then retracting them), unreasonable behavior (failure to leave the abuser, the compulsion to continue engaging with the violent relationship), dangerous intentions (hidden motivations for seeking legal redress): with the convergence of these elements, the experience of violence in intimate relationships becomes something that is recognized by the law, referenced by an article of the Criminal Code, but often not legally acted upon. Marked by frequent acquittals and a widely recognized difficulty in prosecuting, domestic violence becomes a sort of non-evident fact.

The difficulty of identifying the crime resides not only in the lack of charges laid by plaintiffs, or in the lack of evidence, but also in the fact that the flawed subject, the subject that does not behave as expected, is the victim and not the accused. She is responsible for not having avoided the violence, for not having defended herself, for not having pressed charges, for not having understood that what she endured was considered to be violence; in short, for not living up to being a free subject with rights. This focus on the victim's subjectivity, as a crucial point in the demonstration of evidence, entails a constant referral back to her (familiar) story. The required avowal, an admission or acknowledgment, shifts into a requirement to confess wrongdoing. Avowing is an appealing mode in popular culture as much as in legal proceedings. Given that "in today's inquiries, as in the proto-inquiries Foucault dredges up from obscure corners of European cultural and legal history, the search for true facts is inextricable from the search for moral truth and the consequent assignation of responsibility" (Valverde 2017: 143), what does it mean to refuse the demand to tell the truth about oneself? Can there be another subjectivation, starting from the refusal to talk about oneself, or to talk about oneself as expected? Are there different—also, non-verbal—ways of declaring one's condition? How can you be true to yourself and your own deepest feelings (love, suffering, intimacy) without being judged responsible for your own condition? What should a woman tell that has not already been told? The whole complex I have called *speaking violence* in the face of institutions deploys narratives that do not necessarily imply either the depth of experience or the neutral statement of facts. This opposition does not hold. If the multiple processes of truth-telling are better companions for feminism than absolute truth, what about the sphere of justice?

Gender violence is a violence with no witnesses, not only because women have difficulties in testifying, or because there are often no other witnesses available, but also because witnesses tell something that is already known. The subject of this violence is a subject already identified, but that nonetheless, in its modes of giving testimony, reveals itself to institutions in unexpected ways. In this respect, the unexpected should be disentangled from the radical event. The language of radicality has often marginalized women. The feminist subject has been theorized as a subject that irrupts into linear time. Yet it is an immanent irruption, something already there, an everyday event, that belongs to a radical present (Lonzi 1974). Only by taking into account this chance, by insisting on what has been and is constantly told, can the testimony of women be approached ethnographically.

Trial practices and probative regimes, as constitutive processes of objectification and subjectification, are sites where both the facts being spoken and the speaking subjects are generated. Here, I have approached the legal field as a system of knowledge and power that deploys techniques of subjection and subjectivation. I have tried to present this mechanism in all of its complexity and apparent contradiction, showing how the logic of the law intersects with other institutions concerned with advocacy, social services, and security, in order to define the legitimacy of a subject who is the victim of violence. The normativity of the legal system's requirements becomes caught up with the confessional device, so as to render women's testimony inadequate in its essence. Every discipline contains true and false propositions within its bounds yet works to expel beyond its margins an entire "teratology of knowledge" that does not belong in the realm of truth (Foucault 1981: 60). In this respect, women and their testimony embody a monstrosity that evades the discipline of the law. Women are too victimlike, too passive and confused, or conversely too precise, aware, strategic, or agentive. Sometimes they are both at once. Antiheroic, contradictory creatures, they often stand outside the bounds of required congruity. Some form of lack or excess is always attributed to women's words. The eccentric accounts reported here take the attribution of excess to an extreme, producing unexpected deviations of representation. This brings into play different logics and potential ruptures in an order that seems to trap them in an obligatory (and failing) choice between the victim-subject and the agent-subject, between the authentic identity and the constitutive non-authenticity (constructed and manipulative) of the female gender. Detachment from oneself, as a requirement of political resistance, coexists with other forms of subjectivity. The notion of a transparently self-reflecting subject is only one of many possibilities for the expression of experience.

The law can say everything and its opposite on this possibly oblique authenticity. When it comes to the persuasiveness of intimacy and the truth of the self, it is no longer the credibility of witnesses that is in question. The authenticity and intimacy of their experience, the self-awareness involved, falls outside the legal dimension. This has disruptive, profanatory, and unpredictable consequences. In a trial on intimate partner violence, unexpected statements by the victim face a court that might sometimes recognize them and sometimes might in fact not. Those legible as acts of insubordination towards the requests of power emerge as non-linear, incomplete, risky practices. They wrong-foot the interrogation of truth, creating something that justice cannot take on. In a word, they are unjudgable.

A peculiar form of acknowledgment of this incongruous subject re-emerges at times in the words and attitudes of those who deal daily with domestic violence. Relying on the recognition of resonances instead of concrete evidence, on the words of social workers and magistrates, dynamics in court reveal how participants try to engage the possible meanings of experiences by investigating those elements that cannot be determined on the basis of the evidence: shared meaning, dependency, disillusionment, and ambivalence. Common knowledge, experiences, and perceptions of gender and intimate relationships affect the work of judgment. Judgment is both aesthetic and moral. It asserts a distance and yet, at the same time, must show recognition. The quality of a judgment depends neither on an absolute independence from context, nor on the power relations at play, nor on a rigid application of the norms: "[T]o speak justly, [justice] must have hesitated" (Latour 2010: 152). Every relationship between word and experience has its own demand for evidence. The intimate dimension comprises trauma and associated processes of self-governance and self-reflexivity. The dimension of law establishes parameters of truthfulness through the procedural construction of the *prova*. And ethnography requires *evidenza*, the persuasiveness of that which is evident. These different ways of understanding evidence are familiar with the process of hesitation.

Historically, feminism has strived to introduce the unvoiced and unspeakable into public view and debate. It is an archive of the claims and struggles of diverse subjects, all of them unexpected in the terms of normative systems.

This diversity bears an experience that never ceases to re-emerge and to question the forms of knowledge. Its political strength resides in the unpredictability of translating from a language, a stance, a *témoignage*, a form of life, into unforeseen possibilities of change. Different practices of truth-telling may exist as much as different kinds of selves. The refusal to investigate causality can be one of these practices. Rather than an aesthetics of revelation and discovery, the reciprocal mimicry of feminism and anthropology means these remain committed to each other precisely in virtue of their potentially incompatible and unfinished relationship. This relationship also entails an ethics of knowledge. Connecting anthropological and feminist thought is a project of juxtaposition and of partial or fractal connection, where feminist anthropology does not provide a super-context (Moutu 2015). Recent attempts to rethink anthropological knowledge have singled out the capacity of feminist anthropology to reveal decisive political and theoretical issues, by deploying the analytical stance of non-completeness (Holbraad and Pedersen 2017: 143). Ethnographic practice implies a disruption, an interruption of self in the presence of different subjectivities that produces unfamiliar and partial associations: a productive hesitation, a contradiction not to be solved dialectically, where diverse elements are held together in working compatibility (Strathern 2004). In a similar vein, reflexive and normative knowledges, interdependent modes of thinking, constitutive both of legal and anthropological reasoning, are not of the same order and do not occupy a single plane, each slipping into the other (Riles 1994: 648). Tension is the feature of their relationship.

An ethnography of devices for the management of domestic violence and the production of the legal figure of the victim provides an opportunity to account for hesitations in a framework where the law and institutions cannot afford the ambiguity that is claimed in anthropological reflection. Judges cannot not make judgments, social workers cannot

not carry out their services, the police cannot not intervene. Negotiations and hesitations emerge from all sides: from abused women, from social services, from judges themselves, all working with a field that, far from being given, is extremely unstable. Hesitation does not necessarily represent an impasse. Hesitation entails a pause that in turn allows for taking a stance. Disentangling evidence, gender, and intimacy in the dynamics that certify domestic violence affords a better understanding of how judges, professionals, advocates, and claimants aim at "getting it right" both through and despite the legal system. The paradox of women's experience and its avowal, constitutive of intimate partner abuse, could represent a perspective for further investigating the politics of truth-telling. It could open the way to understanding not only the women who testify their truth, but also, significantly, those who do not wish to talk at all before the law. They do not recognize institutions because they are misrecognized by them. These are subjects haunting justice.

References

Abraham, Margaret. 2000. *Speaking the Unspeakable: Marital Violence among South Asian Immigrants in the United States*. New Brunswick: Rutgers University Press.

Abu-Lughod, Lila. 2002. "Do Muslim Women Really Need Saving? Anthropological Reflections on Cultural Relativism and Its Others." *American Anthropologist* 104 (3): 783-790. https://doi.org/10.1525/aa.2002.104.3.783.

Adelman, Madelaine. 2004. "The Battering State: Towards a Political Economy of Domestic Violence." *Journal of Poverty* 8 (3): 45-64. https://doi.org/10.1300/J134v08n03_03.

Agamben, Giorgio. 2005. *Profanazioni*. Roma: Nottetempo.

Archer, John. 2000. "Sex Differences in Aggression between Heterosexual Partners: A Meta-analytic Review." *Psychological Bulletin* 126: 651-680. https://doi.org/10.1037/0033-2909.126.5.651.

Arcidiacono, Davide, and Stefania Crocitti. 2015. "Criminal Justice System Responses to Intimate Partner Violence: The Italian Case." *Criminology & Criminal Justice* 15 (5): 613-632. https://doi.org/10.1177/1748895815586271.

Bargu, Banu. 2017. "The Silent Exception: Hunger Striking and Lip-Sewing." *Law, Culture and the Humanities*, May 24, 2017: 1-28. https://doi.org/10.1177/1743872117709684.

Belmonti, Maria Grazia. 1980. *Un Processo per Stupro: Dal Programma della Rete Due della Televisione Italiana*. Turin: Einaudi.

Beneduce, Roberto. 2015. "The Moral Economy of Lying: Subjectcraft, Narrative Capital, and Uncertainty in the Politics of Asylum." *Medical Anthropology* 34 (6): 551-571. https://doi.org/10.1080/01459740.2015.1074576.

Berlant, Lauren. 1998. "Intimacy: A Special Issue." *Critical Inquiry* 24 (2): 281-288. https://www.journals.uchicago.edu/doi/10.1086/448875.

———. 1999. "The Subject of True Feeling: Pain, Privacy, and Politics." In *Cultural Pluralism, Identity Politics, and the Law*, edited by Austin Sarat and Thomas R. Kearns, 49-84. Ann Arbor: University of Michigan Press.

———. 2008. *The Female Complaint. The Unfinished Business of Sentimentality in American Culture*. Durham: Duke University Press. https://doi.org/10.1215/9780822389163.

Berns, Sandra. 1999. *To Speak as a Judge: Difference, Voice and Power*. Aldershot: Ashgate.

Berti, Daniela, Anthony Good and Giles Tarabout, eds. 2015. *Of Doubt and Proof: Ritual and Legal Practices of Judgment*. London: Routledge.

Beske, Melissa. 2016. *Intimate Partner Violence and Advocate Response: Redefining Love in Western Belize*. Lanham: Lexington Books.

Biehl, João, Byron Good, and Arthur Kleimann, eds. 2007. *Subjectivity: Ethnographic Investigations*. Berkeley: University of California Press.

Bohmer, Carol, and Amy Shuman. 2018. *Political Asylum Deceptions: The Culture of Suspicion*. London: Palgrave Macmillan.

Boni, Stefano. 2012. "Institutional Alignment: The Anniversary of Italy's 150 Years of Unity." *Anthropology Today* 28 (1): 6-10. https://doi.org/10.1111/j.1467-8322.2012.00848.x.

Boltanski, Luc. 1993. *La Souffrance à Distance: Morale Humanitaire, Médias et Politique*. Paris: Éditions Métailié.

Boiano, Ilaria. 2015. *Femminismo e Processo Penale*. Roma: Ediesse.

Bourdieu, Pierre. 1982. *Ce Que Parler Veut Dire: L'Économie des Échanges Linguistiques*. Paris: Fayard.

Bourgois, Philippe. 1995. *In Search of Respect: Selling Crack in El Barrio.* Cambridge: Cambridge University Press.

Broch-Due, Vigdis, and Margit Ystanes, eds. 2016. *Trusting and Its Tribulations. Interdisciplinary Engagements with Intimacy, Sociality and Trust*. New York: Berghahn Books.

Brown, Laura S. 1995. "Not Outside the Range: One Feminist Perspective on Psychic Trauma". In *Trauma. Explorations in* Memory, edited by Cathy Caruth, 100-112. Baltimore: Johns Hopkins University Press.

Brown, Wendy. 2000. "Suffering Rights as Paradoxes." *Constellations* 7 (2): 208-229. https://doi.org/10.1111/1467-8675.00183.

Busatta, Sandra. 2006. "Honour and Shame in the Mediterranean." *Antrocom* 2 (2): 75-78. http://www.antrocom.net/upload/sub/antrocom/020206/04-Antrocom.pdf.

Butler, Judith. 1997a. *The Psychic Life of Power: Theories in Subjection*. Stanford: Stanford University Press.

———. 1997b. *Excitable Speech: A Politics of the Performative.* London: Routledge.

———. 2016. "Afterword." In *Before and After Gender: Sexual Mythologies of Everyday Life*, by Marilyn Strathern, 293-302. Chicago: HAU Books.

Cabot, Heath. 2016. "'Refugee Voices': Tragedy, Ghosts, and the Anthropology of Not Knowing." *Journal of Contemporary Ethnography* 45 (6): 645-672. https://doi.org/10.1177/0891241615625567.

Calasso, Francesco. 1958. *Enciclopedia del Diritto*. Milano: Giuffrè Editore.

Carey, Matthew. 2017. *Mistrust: An Ethnographic Theory*. Chicago: HAU Books.

Caruth, Cathy, ed. 1995. *Trauma: Explorations in Memory*. Baltimore: Johns Hopkins University Press.

———. 1996. *Unclaimed Experience: Trauma, Narrative, and History*. Baltimore: Johns Hopkins University Press.

Casa delle donne per non subire violenza. 2018. *I Femicidi in Italia*. Bologna: Casa delle donne.

Cavina, Marco. 2011. *Nozze di Sangue. Storia della Violenza Coniugale*. Roma-Bari: Laterza.

Chakrabarty, Dipesh. 2000. *Provincializing Europe: Postcolonial Thought and Historical Difference*. Princeton: Princeton University Press.

Charlesworth, Hilary. 1999. "Feminist Methods in International Law." *The American Journal of International Law* 93 (2): 379-394. https://doi.org/10.2307/2997996.

Chiu, Elaine. 2001. "Confronting the Agency in Battered Mothers." *Southern California Law Review* 74 (5): 1223-1273.

Chow, Rey. 1992. "Postmodern Automatons." In *Feminists Theorize the Political*, edited by Judith Butler and Joan W. Scott, 101–117. New York: Routledge.

Christie, Nils. 1986. "The Ideal Victim." In *From Crime Policy to Victim Policy: Reorienting the Justice System*, edited by Ezzat A. Fattah, 17-30. London: Macmillan.

Clifford, James. 1988. *The Predicament of Culture: Twentieth Century Ethnography, Literature, and Art*. Cambridge: Harvard University Press.

Conley, John M., and William M. O'Barr. 1990. *Rules Versus Relationships: The Ethnography of Legal Discourse*. Chicago: University of Chicago Press.

Connell, Patricia. 1997. "Understanding Victimization and Agency: Considerations of Race, Class and Gender." *Political and Legal Anthropology Review* 20 (2): 115-143. https://doi.org/10.1525/pol.1997.20.2.115.

Costa, Diogo, Joaquim Soares, Jutta Lindert, Eleni Hatzidimitriadou, Örjan Sundin, Olga Toth, Elli Ioannidi-Kapolo, and Henrique Barros. 2015. "Intimate Partner Violence: A Study in Men and Women from Six European

Countries." *International Journal of Public Health*, 60 (2): 467-478. https://doi.org/10.1007/s00038-015-0663-1.

Counts, Dorothy Ayers, Judith K. Brown, and Jacquelyn C. Campbell. 1999. *To Have and To Hit: Cultural Perspectives on Wife Beating*. Urbana: University of Illinois Press.

Cowan, Sharon. 2007. "'Freedom and Capacity to Make a Choice:' A Feminist Analysis of Consent in the Criminal Law of Rape." In *Sexuality and the Law: Feminist Engagements,* edited by Vanessa E. Munro and Carl F. Stychin, 51-71. Abingdon, Oxon: Routledge.

Creazzo, Giuditta, ed. 2013. *Se Le Donne Chiedono Giustizia: Le Risposte del Sistema Penale alle Donne Che Subiscono Violenza Nelle Relazioni di Intimità: Ricerca e Prospettive Internazionali*. Bologna: Il Mulino.

Crenshaw, Kimberlé Williams. 1994. "Mapping the Margins: Intersectionality, Identity Politics, and Violence Against Women of Color." In *The Public Nature of Private Violence: Women and the Discovery of Abuse,* edited by Martha Albertson Fineman and Roxanne Mykitiuk, 93-120. New York: Routledge.

Csordas, Thomas J. 2004. "Evidence Of and For What?" *Anthropological Theory* 4 (4): 473-480. https://doi.org/10.1177/1463499604047922.

D'Amelia, Marina. 2005. *La Mamma*. Bologna: Il Mulino.

Daston, Lorraine. 1994. "Marvelous Facts and Miraculous Evidence in Early Modern Europe." In *Questions of Evidence. Proof, Practice, and Persuasion across the Disciplines,* edited by James Chandler, Arnold I. Davidson, and Harry D. Harootunian, 243-274. Chicago: University of Chicago Press.

Das, Veena. 2007. *Life and Words: Violence and the Descent into the Ordinary*. Berkeley: University of California Press.

———. 2008. "Violence, Gender, and Subjectivity." *Annual Review of Anthropology* 37: 283-299. https://doi.org/10.1146/annurev.anthro.36.081406.094430.

———, Arthur Kleinman, Mamphela Ramphele and Pamela Reynolds, eds. 2000. *Violence and Subjectivity*. Berkeley: University of California Press.

De Filippo, Eduardo. 1964. *Filumena Marturano*. Torino: Einaudi.

Demaria, Cristina. 2003. *Teorie di Genere: Femminismo, Critica Postcoloniale e Semiotica*. Milano: Bompiani.

Dobash, Russell P., and R. Emerson Dobash. 2004. "Women's Violence to Men in Intimate Relationships: Working on a Puzzle." *The British Journal of Criminology* 44 (3): 324-349. https://doi.org/10.1093/bjc/azh026.

Dominguez, Virginia R., ed. 2013. *Violence: Anthropologists Engaging Violence: 1980-2012. American Anthropologist*. https://anthrosource.onlinelibrary.wiley.com/doi/toc/10.1002/(ISSN)1548-1433(CAT)VirtualIssues(VI)violence.

Eckert, Julia. 2016. "Does #Evidence Matter?" *Allegra Lab*. November 8, 2016. http://allegralaboratory.net/does-evidence-matter/.

Edwards, Jeanette, and Marilyn Strathern. 2000. "Including your Own." In *Cultures of Relatedness: New Approaches to the Study of Kinship*, edited by Janet Carsten, 149-66. Cambridge: Cambridge University Press.

EURES Ricerche Economiche e Sociali. 2015. *III Rapporto su Caratteristiche, Dinamiche e Profili di Rischio del Femminicidio in Italia*. 2015. Rome: Eures. http://www.quotidianosanita.it/allegati/allegato4803121.pdf.

Fassin, Didier. 2008. "The Humanitarian Politics of Testimony: Subjectification through Trauma in the Israeli–Palestinian Conflict." *Cultural Anthropology* 3 (3): 531-558. https://doi.org/10.1111/j.1548-1360.2008.00017.x.

———. 2013. "The Precarious Truth of Asylum." *Public Culture* 25 (1): 39-63. https://doi.org/10.1215/08992363-1890459.

———, and Estelle D'Halluin. 2007. "Critical Evidence: The Politics of Trauma in French Asylum Policies." *Ethos* 35 (3): 300-329.

———, and Richard Rechtman. 2007. *L'empire du Traumatisme: Enquête sur la Condition de la Victime*. Paris: Flammarion.

Felman, Shoshana. 2002. *Juridical Unconscious: Trials and Traumas in the Twentieth Century*. Cambridge: Harvard University Press.

Foucault, Michel. 1975. *Surveiller et Punir: Naissance de la Prison*. Paris: Gallimard.

———. 1978. *The History of Sexuality*, Vol. 1. New York: Pantheon.

———. 1981. "The Order of Discourse." In *Untying the Text: A Post-Structuralist Reader*, edited by R. Young, 48-79. Boston: Routledge and Kegan Paul.

———. 2001. *Dits et Écrits: Tome 2, 1976-1988*. Paris: Gallimard.

———. 2010. *The Government of Self and Others*. Edited by Frédéric Gros, François Ewald, and Alessandro Fontana. Translated by Graham Burchell. New York: Picador.

———. 2014. *Wrong-Doing, Truth-Telling: The Function of Avowal in Justice*. Edited by Fabienne Brion and Bernard E. Harcourt. Translated by Stephen W. Sawyer. Chicago: University of Chicago Press.

Foisneau, Lise. 2016. "La Crainte des Roms: Pratiques Romanès de la Défiance." *Tracés* 31 (2): 87-108. https://doi.org/10.4000/traces.6714.

Fricker, Miranda. 2007. *Epistemic Injustice. Power and the Ethics of Knowing*. Oxford: Oxford University Press.

Garapon, Antoine. 1997. *Bien Juger: Essai sur le Rituel Judiciaire*. Paris: Odile Jacob

Geertz, Clifford. 1983. *Local Knowledge. Further Essays in Interpretative Anthropology*. New York: Basic Books.

Geschiere, Peter. 2013. *Witchcraft, Intimacy, and Trust: Africa in Comparison*. Chicago: University of Chicago Press.

Giddens, Anthony. 1992. *The Transformation of Intimacy: Sexuality, Love, and Eroticism in Modern Societies*. Stanford: Stanford University Press.

Giordano, Cristiana. 2015. "Lying the Truth: Practices of Confession and Recognition." *Current Anthropology* 56 (S12): S211-S221. https://www.journals.uchicago.edu/doi/pdf/10.1086/683272.

Gissi, Alessandra. 2010. "Il Corpo della Nazione in Festa: Alcune Considerazioni su Genere e Comunicazione in Occasione dei 150 Anni dell'Unità d'Italia." *Genesis* 9 (2): 221-228.

Goldstein, Donna M. 2003. *Laughter Out of Place: Race, Class, Violence, and Sexuality in a Rio Shantytown*. Berkeley: University of California Press.

Good, Anthony. 2007. *Anthropology and Expertise in the Asylum Courts*. Abingdon, Oxon: Routledge-Cavendish.

Graeber, David. 2012. "Dead Zones of the Imagination: On Violence, Bureaucracy, and Interpretive Labor." *HAU: Journal of Ethnographic Theory* 2 (2): 105-28. https://doi.org 10.14318/hau2.2.007.

Greenhouse, Carol J. 1995. "Reading Violence." In *Law's Violence*, edited by Austin Sarat and Thomas R. Kearns, 105-139. Ann Arbor: The University of Michigan Press.

———. 2017. "The Scale(s) of Justice." In *Redescribing Relations: Strathernian Conversations on Ethnography, Knowledge and Politics,* edited by Ashley Lebner, 62-73. New York: Berghahn Books.

Gribaldo, Alessandra. 2014. "The Paradoxical Victim: Intimate Violence Narratives on Trial in Italy." *American Ethnologist* 41 (4): 743-756. https://doi.org/10.1111/amet.12109.

———. 2018. "Veline, Ordinary Women and Male Savages: Disentangling Racism and Heteronormativity in Contemporary Narratives on Sexual Freedom." *Modern Italy* 23 (2): 145-158. 10.1017/MIT.2018.5.

———. 2019a. "Hashtags, Testimonies, and Measurements: Gender Violence and its Interpretation." *Anuac: Journal of the Italian Society of Cultural Anthropology* 8 (1): 7-30. https://doi.org/10.7340/anuac2239-625X-3622.

———. 2019b. "The Burden of Intimate Partner Violence: Evidence, Experience, and Persuasion." *PoLAR: Political and Legal Anthropology Review* 42 (2): 283-297. https://doi.org/10.1111/plar.12309.

Harvey, Penelope and Peter Gow, eds. 1994. *Sex and Violence: Issues in Representation and Experience.* London: Routledge.

Hastrup, Kirsten. 2003. "Violence, Suffering and Human Rights: Anthropological Reflections." *Anthropological Theory* 3 (3): 309-323. https://doi.org/10.1177/14634996030033004.

———. 2004. "Getting it Right. Knowledge and Evidence in Anthropology." *Anthropological Theory* 4 (4): 455-472. https://doi.org/10.1177/1463499604047921.

Hautzinger, Sara. 2007. *Violence in the City of Women: Police and Batterers in Bahia, Brazil.* Berkeley: California University Press.

Hearn, Jeff. 2012. "The Sociological Significance of Domestic Violence: Tensions, Paradoxes and Implications." *Current Sociology* 61 (2): 152-170. https://doi.org/10.1177/0011392112456503.

Herman, Judith Lewis. 1997. *Trauma and Recovery*. New York: Basic Books.

Hinton, Alex. 2012. "Violence." In *A Companion to Moral Anthropology*, edited by Didier Fassin, 500-518. Malden, MA: Wiley-Blackwell.

Hirsch, Susan F. 1998. *Pronouncing and Persevering: Gender and the Discourses of Disputing in an African Islamic Court.* Chicago: University of Chicago Press.

———, and Mindie Lazarus-Black. 1994. "Introduction/Performance and Paradox: Exploring Law's Role in Hegemony and Resistance." In *Contested States: Law,*

Hegemony and Resistance, edited by Mindie Lazarus-Black and Susan Hirsch, 1-34. New York: Routledge.

Holbraad, Martin, and Morten Axel Pedersen. 2017. *The Ontological Turn: An Anthropological Exposition*. Cambridge: Cambridge University Press.

hooks, bell. 1984. *Feminist Theory: From Margin to Center*. Cambridge, MA: South End Press.

Istituto Nazionale di Statistica (Istat). 2015. *La Violenza Contro le Donne Dentro e Fuori la Famiglia*. Rome: Istat.

Jacquemet, Marco. 1996. *Credibility in Court: Communicative Practices in the Camorra Trials*. Cambridge: Cambridge University Press.

Jean-Klein, Iris and Annelise Riles. 2005. "Introducing Discipline: Anthropology and Human Rights Administrations." *PoLAR: Political and Legal Anthropology Review* 28 (2): 173-202. https://www.jstor.org/stable/24497693.

Johnson, Holly, Natalia Ollus, and Sami Nevala. 2008. *Violence against Women: An International Perspective*. New York: Springer.

Johnson, Michael P., and Janel M. Leone. 2005. "The Differential Effects of Intimate Terrorism and Situational Couple Violence: Findings from the National Violence Against Women Survey." *Journal of Family Issues* 26 (3): 322-350. https://doi.org/10.1177/0192513X04270345.

Kapila, Kriti. 2013. "...in South Asia." *HAU: Journal of Ethnographic Theory* 3 (2): 299–304. https://doi.org/10.14318/hau3.2.020.

Keane, Webb. 2000. "Voice." *Journal of Linguistic Anthropology* 9 (1-2): 271-273. https://doi.org/10.1525/jlin.1999.9.1-2.271.

Kimmel, Michael S. 2002. "'Gender Symmetry in Domestic Violence: A Substantive and Methodological Research Review." *Violence Against Women* 8 (11): 1332-1363. https://doi.org/10.1177/107780102237407.

Kirmayer, J. Lawrence. 2007. "Failures of Imagination: The Refugee's Predicament." In *Understanding Trauma*, edited by J. L. Kirmayer, R. Lemelson and M. Barad, 363-38. Cambridge: Cambridge University Press.

Kleinman, Arthur, Veena Das, and Margaret Lock, eds. 1997. *Social Suffering*. Berkeley: University of California Press.

Kobelinsky, Carolina. 2015. "Emotions as Evidence: Hearings in the French Asylum Court." In *On Doubt and Proof: Ritual and Legal Practices of Judgment*, edited by Daniela Berti, Anthony Good, and Giles Tarabout, 163-182. London: Routledge.

Lacey, Nicola. 2002. "Violence, Ethics, and Law: Feminist Reflections on a Familiar Dilemma." In *Visible Women: Essays on Feminist Legal Theory and Political Philosophy,* edited by Susan James and Stephanie Palmer, 117-135. Oregon: Hart Publishing.

Latour, Bruno. 2010. *The Making of Law: An Ethnography of the Conseil d'Etat*. Cambridge: Polity Press.

Lazarus-Black, Mindie. 2007. *Everyday Harm: Domestic Violence, Court Rites, and Cultures of Reconciliation*. Urbana: University of Illinois Press.

Le Guin, Ursula K. 2012. *Earthsea Cycle: Tehanu.* New York: Atheneum Books.

Lonzi, Carla. 1974. *Sputiamo su Hegel e Altri Scritti*, Milano: Scritti di Rivolta Femminile.

Mahoney, Martha. 1994. "Victimization or Oppression? Women's Lives, Violence, and Agency." In *The Public Nature of Private Violence,* edited by Martha Albertson Fineman and Roxanne Mykitiuk. New York: Routledge.

Mathieu, Nicole-Claude. 1999. "Bourdieu ou le Pouvoir Auto-hypnotique de la Domination Masculine." *Les Temps Modernes*, 604: 286-324.

Matoesian, Gregory M. 1993. *Reproducing Rape: Domination through Talk in the Courtroom*. Chicago: University of Chicago Press.

Malkki, Liisa H. 1996. "Speechless Emissaries: Refugees, Humanitarianism, and Dehistoricization." *Cultural Anthropology* 11 (3): 377-404. https://doi.org/10.1525/can.1996.11.3.02a00050

Maxwell, Lida. 2018. "The Politics and Gender of Truth-telling in Foucault's Lectures on *Parrhesia*." *Contemporary Political Theory* 18: 22-42. https://doi.org 10.1057/S41296-018-0224-5.

McCormick, Charles. T. 1954. *Handbook of the Law of Evidence*. St. Paul, Minn.: West Publishing.

McKinley, Michelle. 1997. "Life Stories, Disclosure and the Law." *PoLAR: Political and Legal Anthropology Review* 20 (2): 70-82. https://doi.org/10.1525/pol.1997.20.2.70.

McClusky, Laura J. 2001. *Here, Our Culture Is Hard: Stories of Domestic Violence from a Mayan Community in Belize*. Austin: University of Texas Press.

McGilligray, Anne, and Brenda Comaskey. 1999. *Black Eyes All of the Time: Intimate Violence, Aboriginal Women, and the Justice System*. Toronto: University of Toronto Press.

Merry, Sally E. 1995. "Gender Violence and Legally Engendered Selves." *Identities: Global Studies in Culture and Power* 2 (1-2): 49-73. https://doi.org/10.1080/1070289X.1997.9962526.

———. 2000. *Colonizing Hawai'i: The Cultural Power of Law*. Princeton: Princeton University Press.

———. 2001. "Spatial Governmentality and the New Urban Social Order: Controlling Gender Violence through Law." *American Anthropologist* 103 (1): 16-29. https://doi.org 10.1525/aa.2001.103.1.16.

———, and Susan Bibler Coutin. 2014. "Technologies of Truth in the Anthropology of Conflict." *American Ethnologist* 41 (1): 1-16. https://doi.org/10.1111/amet.12055.

Mertz, Elizabeth. 1994. "Legal Language: Pragmatics, Poetics, and Social Power." *Annual Review of Anthropology* 23: 435-455. https://doi.org/10.1146/annurev.an.23.100194.002251.

Mills, Linda G. 2003. *Insult to Injury: Rethinking our Responses to Intimate Abuse*. Princeton: Princeton University Press.

Minow, Martha. 1990. *Making all the Difference: Inclusion, Exclusion, and American Law*. Ithaca: Cornell University Press.

Modleski, Tanja. 1991. *Feminism Without Women: Culture and Criticism in a Postfeminist Age*. New York: Routledge.

Mohanty, Chandra. 1984. "Under Western Eyes: Feminist Scholarship and Colonial Discourses." *Boundary 2* 12, no. 3/13 (1): 333-58. https://doi.org/10.2307/302821.

Moore, Henrietta. 1994. "The Problem of Explaining Violence in Social Science." In *Sex and Violence: Issues in Representation and Experience*, edited by Penelope Harvey and Peter Gow, 138-155. London: Routledge.

———. 2007. *The Subject of Anthropology: Gender, Symbolism and Psychoanalysis*. Cambridge: Polity Press.

Moutu, Andrew. 2015. "Apologetics of an Apology and an Apologia." In *Knowledge and Ethics in Anthropology: Obligations and Requirements*, edited by Lisette Josephides, 79-92. London: Bloomsbury.

Mulla, Sameena. 2014. T*he Violence of Care: Rape Victims, Forensic Nurses, and Sexual Assault Intervention*. New York: New York University Press.

Nader, Laura. 2002. *The Life of the Law: Anthropological Projects*. Berkeley: University of California Press.

Oksala, Johanna. 2004. "Anarchic Bodies: Foucault and the Feminist Question of Experience." *Hypatia* 19 (4): 99-121. https://doi.org/10.1111/j.1527-2001.2004.tb00150.x.

Ong, Aihwa. 2003. *Buddha is Hiding: Refugees, Citizenship, the New America*. Berkeley: University of California Press.

Ortner, Sherry B. 2006. *Anthropology and Social Theory: Culture, Power, and the Acting Subject*. Durham: Duke University Press.

Pateman, Carole. 1988. *The Sexual Contract*. Cambridge: Polity Press.

Pitch, Tamar. 2013. *Contro il Decoro. L'uso Politico della Pubblica Decenza*. Roma-Bari: Laterza.

Plaza, Monique. (1978) 1981. "Our Damages and Their Compensation; Rape: The Will Not to Know of Michel Foucault." *Feminist Issues* 1: 25-35. https://doi.org/10.1007/BF02685564.

Plesset, Sonja. 2006. *Sheltering Women: Negotiating Gender and Violence in Northern Italy*. Stanford: Stanford University Press.

Pottage, Alain. 2014. "Law after Anthropology: Object and Technique in Roman Law." *Theory, Culture & Society* 31 (2/3): 147-166. https://doi.org/10.1177/0263276413502239.

Riches, David, ed. 1986. *The Anthropology of Violence*. Oxford: B. Blackwell.

Riles, Annalise. 1994. "Representing In-Between: Law, Anthropology, and the Rhetoric of Interdisciplinarity." *University of Illinois Law Review* 3: 597-649.

Robbins, Joel. 2008. "On Not Knowing Other Minds: Confession, Intention, and Linguistic Exchange in a Papua New Guinea Community." *Anthropology Quarterly* 81 (2): 421-429. https://doi.org/ 10.1353/anq.0.0007.

———, and Alan Rumsey. 2008. "Cultural and Linguistic Anthropology and the Opacity of Other Minds." *Anthropology Quarterly* 81 (2): 407-420. https://doi.org/10.1353/ANQ.0.0007.

Rose, Nicholas. 1989. *Governing the Soul: The Shaping of Private Self*. London: Free Association Books.

Sahlins, Marshall. 2013. *What Kinship Is, and Is Not*. Chicago: University of Chicago Press.

Schneider, Elizabeth M. 1994. "The Violence of Privacy." In *The Public Nature of Private Violence*, edited by Martha Albertson Fineman and Roxanne Mykitiuk, 36-58. New York: Routledge.

Schneider, Jane, ed. 1998. *Italy's "Southern Question": Orientalism in One Country*. Oxford: Berg.

Scott, Joan W. 1991. "The Evidence of Experience." *Critical Enquiry* 17 (4): 773-797. https://doi.org/10.1086/448612.

Sertaç, Sehlikoglu, and Asli Zengin. 2015. "Introduction: Why Revisit Intimacy?" *The Cambridge Journal of Anthropology* 33 (2): 20-25. https://doi.org/10.3167/ca.2015.330203.

Silbey, Susan S. 2008. "Introduction." In *Law and Science, Volume 1: Epistemological, Evidentiary and Relational Engagements*, edited by Susan S. Silbey, xi-xxvii. Burlington: Ashgate.

Smart, Carol. 1989. *Feminism and the Power of Law*. London: Routledge.

Spivak, Gayatri C. 1988. "Can the Subaltern Speak?" In *Marxism and the Interpretation of Culture*, edited by Cary Nelson and Lawrence Grossberg, 271-313. Urbana, Chicago: University of Illinois Press.

Strathern, Marilyn. 1972. *Official and Unofficial Courts: Legal Assumptions and Expectations in a Highlands Community*. New Guinea Research Unit, Australian National University.

———. 1987. "An Awkward Relationship: The Case of Feminism and Anthropology." *Signs* 12 (2): 276-292. https://doi.org/10.1086/494321.

———. 1996. "Cutting the Network." *The Journal of the Royal Anthropological Institute* 2 (3): 517-535. https://doi.org/10.2307/3034901.

———. 1999. *Property Substance and Effect: Anthropological Essays on Persons and Things*. London: The Athlone Press.

———. 2004. *Partial Connections*. Oxford: Altamira Press.

———. 2008. "Old and New Reflections." In *How Do We Know: Evidence, Ethnography, and the Making of Anthropological Knowledge*, edited by Liana Chua, Carey High, and Timm Lau, 20-35. Cambridge: Cambridge Scholars Publishing.

Trinch, Shonna. 2003. *Latinas' Narratives of Domestic Abuse: Discrepant Versions of Violence*. Amsterdam: John Benjamins Publishing Corporation.

———, and Susan Berk-Seligson. 2002. "Narrating in Protective Order Interviews: A Source of Interactional

Troubler." *Language in Society* 31 (3): 383-418. https://doi.org/10.1017/S0047404502020274.

Twining, William. 2006. *Rethinking Evidence: Exploratory Essays*. Cambridge: Cambridge University Press.

Valverde, Mariana. 2004. "Experience and Truth Telling in a Post-Humanist World: A Foucauldian Contribution to Feminist Ethical Reflections." In *Feminism and the Final Foucault*, edited by Dianna Taylor and Karen Vintges, 67-90. Urbana: University of Illinois Press.

———. 2017. *Michel Foucault*. London: Routledge.

Virgilio, Maria. 2016. "Nuovo Lessico per il Diritto pPenale: Le Vittime della Violenza di Genere Contro le Donne." In *Scritti in Onore di Luigi Stortoni,* edited by Michele Caianiello, Francesca Curi, Marco Mantovani, Silvia Tordini Cagli, and Valeria Torre. Bologna: Bononia University Press.

Viveiros de Castro, Eduardo, and Carlos Fausto. 2017. "Within the Limits of a Certain Language: Interview with Marilyn Strathern." In *Redescribing Relations: Strathernian Conversations on Ethnography, Knowledge and Politics,* edited by Ashley Lebner, 39-62. New York: Berghahn Books.

Walker, Lenore E. A. 2000. *The Battered Woman Syndrome*. New York: Springer Publishing Company.

Websdale, Neil. 1998. *Rural Woman Battering and the Justice System: An Ethnography*. Thousand Oaks, CA: Sage.

White, Lucie E. 1990. "Subordination, Rhetorical Survival Skills, and Sunday Shoes: Notes on the Hearings of Mr. G." *Buffalo Law Review* 38 (1): 1-58. https://digitalcommons.law.buffalo.edu/buffalolawreview/vol38/iss1/3.

Wies, Jennifer R., and Hillary J. *Haldane.* 2011. *Anthropology at the Front Lines of Gender-Based Violence.* Nashville: Vanderbilt University Press.